TABLE OF CONTENTS

INTRODUCTION

In the introduction to his 2012 National Strategic Guidance, "Sustaining U.S. Global Leadership: Priorities for the 21st Century Defense," the President of the United States declared, "We are a nation in a moment of transition." The withdrawal of United States forces from Iraq is complete, Osama Bin Laden was located and killed, and in the President's determination, enough progress had occurred in Afghanistan to begin the transition to Afghani responsibility. Simultaneously, a full-fledged budget crisis is exacerbating the complex conditions of this transition. The combination of these factors has resulted in Presidential direction and a legislative mandate to reduce federal spending that include deep cuts in the Department of Defense budget.[1] Despite the legislative requirement to reduce defense spending by almost half a trillion dollars, both President Obama and the Secretary of Defense Leon Panetta stressed the need to ensure that we maintain the ability to prevail in the cyber domain. Secretary Panetta stressed, "…we will protect, and in some cases increase, our investments in special operations forces, in new technologies like ISR and unmanned systems, in space – and, in particular, in cyberspace – capabilities."[2] In a 60 Minutes interview in December 2011, Secretary Panetta articulated the seriousness of the cyber threat and explained why this investment is critical for the security of our nation: "The reality is that there is the cyber capability to

---

[1] U.S. Department of Defense. *Sustaining U.S. Global Leadership: Priorities for 21st Century Defense.* (Washington DC: Department of Defense, 5 January 2012), Presidential Cover Letter.

[2] Zachary Keck. "Panetta: Cyber attack could paralyze our country," Examiner.com, http://www.examiner.com/foreign-policy-in-washington-dc/panetta-cyber-attack-could-paralyze-our-country (accessed January 7, 2012)

basically bring down our power grid… to paralyze our financial system in this country… to virtually paralyze our country."[3]

Despite the recognition of the cyber threat by the President and Secretary of Defense as articulated in speeches and in the capstone national strategic guidance documents, there has been a lack of critical analysis regarding the truly unique capabilities of cyber technology. Indeed, advances in cyber technology have fostered a military revolution that has radically changed the future of warfare. This revolution requires a framework of war that will provide an underpinning that will guide the employment of our strategic capabilities *in both the physical and virtual domains*. This thesis examines how the cyber military revolution has caused a conceptual gap between the current and necessary framework of war and how cyber technology is influencing that framework.

The underpinning of the current United States framework of war comes from the Prussian military strategist Carl von Clausewitz. His theory characterizes war as the shifting interplay between a trinity of forces: passion; chance and probability; and reason, most commonly referred to as the people; the commander and his army; and the government. However, Clausewitz formulated his theory in the first quarter of the nineteenth century over 125 years before the invention of the digital computer and the beginnings of the Internet. This thesis will illustrate how the introduction of the virtual cyber domain has resulted in challenges, complexities, and necessary changes to the framework of war that Clausewitz could not have foreseen in the early 19th century as he authored his influential and still valuable work, *On War*.

---

[3] Ibid.

With the low cost and limited, if any, barriers to entry into the cyber domain, an increasing number of actors have the ability to attack with virtual weapons that have more flexibility than seen in the history of warfare.[4] This flexibility, supported by the open cyber domain, allows diverse actors to challenge and attempt to thwart United States' interests and operations by injecting continual confusion, ambiguity, and disorder into the strategic environment at the speed of light. Therefore, an effective framework of war in the cyber age requires a foundational theory that guides understanding and synthesizes chaotic, complex, and often contradictory information faster than one's opponent.[5] Colonel John Boyd's Observe-Orient-Decide-Act (OODA) loop is a synthesis of various theories of warfare. OODA has extensive domain of applicability that can address the means to identify, distill, and prevail over the challenges the cyber domain presents to the strategic environment. This thesis will outline the development and key aspects of Boyd's theory to illustrate how it can provide the necessary core element for a new framework of war.

There is an immediate need for this new framework of war. The United States is indeed in a period of transition with the conclusion of combat operations in Iraq and the acceleration of transitional activities in Afghanistan. The stage is now set for the potential conclusion of the longest-running armed conflict in our nation's history. However, there is also growing recognition that the conclusion of operations in Iraq and Afghanistan will not complete or define this period of transition. The United States has been involved in an unseen third war that is escalating and expanding daily. This unseen

---

[4] Kenneth Geers, "Sun Tzu and Cyber War," Cooperative Cyber Defence Centre of Excellence, http://www.ccdcoe.org/articles/2011/Geers_SunTzuandCyberWar.pdf, (Accessed February 16, 2012).

[5] James King, "OODA Loops for fighter pilots, business analysts and testers." Kingsinsight.com, http://kingsinsight.com/2012/02/27/ooda-loops-for-fighter-pilots-business-analysts-and-testers/, (accessed February 27, 2012).

war has the potential to cause significantly more destruction to the military and the public and private sectors than occurred during the deadly attacks on September 11, 2001 or during this last decade of combat operations.

In a *Washington Post* editorial, Admiral Mike McConnell, the former Director of National Intelligence and the National Security Agency, described this third war and provided a blunt assessment of United States' progress in this conflict:

> The United States is fighting a cyber-war today, and we are losing. It is that simple. As the most wired nation on Earth, we offer the most targets of significance, yet our cyber-defenses are woefully lacking. The problem is not one of resources; even in our current fiscal straights, we can afford to upgrade our defenses. The problem is we lack a cohesive strategy to meet this challenge.[6]

In August of 2006, Major General William Lord of the Air Force Cyberspace Command disclosed that the first "virtual" shots of a cyber war against United States military information systems occurred as early as 1998.[7] For over a decade, the Chinese and Russians have been exploiting vulnerabilities in United States government and military networks as well as in private networks of leading defense contractors. Their efforts have had a devastating economic and budgetary impact that will ultimately threaten the operational capability and safety of our nation's combat forces. For example, the United States Navy invested almost $5 billion dollars to develop a quiet electric drive to increase the survivability of its submarine forces and in a separate program spent billions to develop a radar upgrade for the Aegis class cruiser fleet. The

---

[6] Mike McConnell. "Mike McConnell on how to win the cyber war we're losing," Washington Post. http://www.washingtonpost.com/wp-dyn/content/article/2010/02/25/AR2010022502493.html (accessed January 7, 2012).

[7] Joel Brenner, *America the Vulnerable: Inside the New Threat Matrix of Digital Espionage, Crime and Warfare* (New York: Penguin Press, 2011), 3.

Chinese were able to target both of those specific systems and steal detailed program information through government-protected information systems.[8]

The lack of a comprehensive framework of war to deal with threats occurring across the physical and virtual domains, coupled with the weaknesses of current United States cyber defenses, has allowed the damages to include and go beyond the military sector. These types of multi-domain attacks, operations, and threats are not a future possibility. The example below shows that such events have already occurred on a massive scale, creating an impact that was exponentially devastating. Does our Joint Doctrine address this type of challenge? When do actions in cyber cross the threshold of war? How will the world community in general and the United States in particular combat these future threats?

On May 25, 2009, North Korea conducted a successful underground nuclear weapons test, signaling its desired entry into the nuclear club. This success also highlighted that a decade and a half of diplomatic efforts designed to prevent this from occurring had failed. Several strategists believe this unprecedented escalation of saber-rattling was due to a perceived need by North Korea's Supreme Leader Kim Jong-il to provide a stronger indication of what might happen if the pace and frequency of the normal concessions of loans, free food, and oil was not increased. These types of concessions to North Korea by the United States and our regional partners had been the historical incentive used to attempt to modify North Korean behavior and resume discussions to reduce elevated tensions on the Korean peninsula.[9]

---

[8] Ibid., 3.

[9] Richard A. Clark and Robert K. Knake. *Cyber War: The Next Threat to National Security and What to do About it* (New York: Harper Collins, 2010), 22.

The actions directed by Supreme Leader Kim Jong-il did not have the desired strategic or economic effects he was attempting to achieve. The Obama administration decided to implement a new approach to North Korean provocative actions, and elected not to respond with the typical concessions. Instead, the United States verbally condemned the nuclear test and announced they would base defensive missiles in Hawaii as a deterrent and counter-measure to North Korean actions and growing capabilities.[10]

As the 2009 Independence Day celebrations began in Washington D.C., North Korea responded to the shift in approach by the Obama administration with a simultaneous show of force in the physical domain and an attack in the virtual domain. The show of force consisted of the launch of seven short-range ballistic missiles into the Sea of Japan. Prior to the launches, a virtual attack started when the transmission of a botnet virus message to approximately 40,000 computers occurred. The virus, attributed by South Korean analysts as coming from a North Korean agent, directed the infected computers to start a Distributed Denial of Service (DDOS) cyber attack on a list of United States and South Korean government, military, and international company computer systems.[11]

The DDOS attack brought down the United States Departments of Homeland Security and State's unclassified computer systems, and eventually expanded to the capability of sending out as many as one million requests per second that crashed the servers at the Treasury Department, Secret Service, Federal Trade Commission, and Department of Transportation. The attack also crashed or degraded the servers or websites of the NASDAQ, New York Mercantile, New York Stock Exchange, and the

---

[10] Ibid., 22-23.
[11] Ibid., 23.

Washington Post, demonstrating that the public and private sector are vulnerable and not immune to a cyber attack.[12]

A separate variant of the botnet virus also initially infected between 30,000 and 60,000 computers that directly targeted South Korean government and bank computers. This part of the attack was not simply a worm computer virus released into the cyber domain to replicate and infect as many systems as autonomously possible; it was actively controlled and modified to direct an estimated 166,000 computers from seventy-four countries in an attempt to overwhelm South Korean fiber-optic cables and routers leading out of the country. Pentagon analysts later concluded the purpose of this attack in the virtual domain was most likely a test by North Korea to see if they could overload and cutoff South Korea's Internet connection to the rest of the world. The United States relies on those connections to support the computer system and communications infrastructure necessary for daily military operations and to coordinate the logistics required to reinforce our forces in the event of a crisis on the Korean peninsula.[13]

The Chinese cyber espionage and theft of vital information on the United States Navy's submarine electric drive and Aegis radar upgrade, coupled with North Korean actions in the physical and virtual domains during the 2009 Independence Day weekend, are two examples that demonstrate the changes in the conduct of warfare that were made possible by the cyber military revolution. The North Korean cyber attacks on critical United States transportation and banking infrastructure demonstrates the need for a new framework of war that can address the blurring boundary between war and peace.

---

[12] Ibid., 24.
[13] Ibid., 25-29.

The relationship between the military and society is in the midst of a transformation caused by the revolutionary impact of cyber technology that is reshaping cultures, redefining how nations conduct business, and causing significant organizational transformation within the world's armed forces. As highlighted by the President and Secretary of Defense, investment and prioritization of the development of our cyber capabilities is necessary to ensure we have the ability to fight and secure the virtual battlefields. Failure to address and to resource properly our ability to dominate in the virtual domain threatens our nation's economic engine and will allow attacks that can directly or indirectly threaten the development, safety, and combat effectiveness of the United States military. Further, as the North Korean attack demonstrated, the cyber military revolution has changed the balance between offense and defense. Offensive cyber operations are difficult to deter, detect, and defeat and provide the virtual ways and means to affect our ability to conduct operations in and across the physical domains of land, sea, air, and space. As this increased offensive capability becomes more widely available, it is reinforcing the need for a revised framework of war that can address these new and developing challenges.

Chapter 1 of this thesis will provide an analysis of this latest military revolution in order to highlight the changes cyber technology has introduced into the framework and future of warfare. This analysis will set the foundation required for the assessment in Chapter 2 of the applicability of continuing to use Clausewitz's framework of war for foundational joint doctrine in the cyber era. Chapter 3 will use Colonel John Boyd's OODA loop to provide the necessary adjustments and the foundational core element for a new United States framework of war. Chapter 4 will conclude by proposing a new foundational framework of war for Joint Doctrine that can guide the development of the strategy and operations necessary to respond and prevail over the challenges that cyber advances have created in the conduct of current and future warfare.

CHAPTER 1: THE CYBER MILITARY REVOLUTION
AND THE FUTURE OF WARFARE

The introduction of the cyber domain has sparked a military revolution that has fundamentally shifted the way the United States, its allies and partners, as well as potential adversaries, will fight current and future wars. Examining previous military revolutions will increase the understanding of what the future of war in the cyber age will look like and how it will develop. The effects of the fundamental changes brought about by each military revolution are additive. A synthesis of the key attributes from each of the military revolutions to date is necessary to determine the key aspects of the cyber military revolution and the degree of impact cyber will have on the future of warfare.

Within United States military strategy and doctrine-development organizations, classifying the seismic changes in the framework of war as military revolutions has grown in popularity over the last twenty years. Military revolutions have occurred when an evaluation of historic and contemporary military operations identifies fundamental changes in the framework of war accompanied by equivalent changes in politics and society.[1] Historians continue to debate how many military revolutions have occurred throughout history; however, there is general consensus on how profound the changes must be to qualify:

> A military revolution, in the fullest sense, occurs only when a new civilization arises to challenge the old, when an entire society transforms itself, forcing its armed services to change at every level simultaneously – from technology and culture to organization, strategy, tactics, training, doctrine and logistics. When this happens, the relationship of the military to the economy

---

[1] MacGregor Knox and Williamson Murray, *The Dynamics of Military Revolution, 1300-2050* (Cambridge: Cambridge University Press, 2001), 6.

and society is transformed and the military balance of power on earth is shattered.[2]

Strategists seeking to determine the impact of the introduction of the cyber domain to warfare need to understand how the theory of military revolutions developed and should be aware of the potential to confuse technological innovation with a military revolution. Focusing on technological innovations and not evaluating any accompanying changes to society, strategy, concepts of operation or doctrine can prevent strategists from identifying whether a true military revolution has occurred. An effective evaluation of a potential military revolution requires the strategist to determine if fundamental strategic changes are necessary or if there is simply a need to match or counter the technological advances within current forces.

The Development of the Concept of Military Revolutions

The conceptual roots of military revolutions come from the writings of British historian Michael Roberts and Soviet military theorists. In 1955, Roberts theorized that changes developed and employed by the Swedish warrior-king Gustavus Adolphus led to an abandonment of the traditional approaches and tactics used by armies throughout Europe. Robert's ideas and theory went unchallenged for nearly twenty years, until historian Geoffrey Parker evaluated and then expanded on the concept of military revolutions. Parker's book, *The Military Revolution: Military Innovation and the Rise of the West 1500-1800* was one of the first of a growing list of books and works delving into the concept of military revolution.[3] These books and scholarly works have sparked

---

[2] Alvin Toffler and Heidi Toffler. *War and Anti-War: Survival at the Dawn of the 21st Century* (New York: Warner Books Inc., 1993), 34.

[3] Bryon Greenwald, "Understanding Change: An Intellectual and Practical Study of Military Innovation-U.S. Army Antiaircraft Artillery and the Battle for Legitimacy, 1917-45" (PhD diss, Ohio State University, 2004)

decades of debate among historians about the nature of military revolutions but more importantly, they have helped to foster a new approach to the evaluation of significant changes in warfare.[4]

Soviet military strategists were the second major influence on the development of the concept of military revolutions. Their contributions provide a historical example on the importance of recognizing when fundamental shifts in the framework of war have occurred.[5] Russia's near defeat at the hands of a messianically driven and technology-infused Nazi Germany fostered a renaissance in the Soviet study of military art and science. Energized by the realization that they had missed a major shift in warfare after World War I – specifically, the growth of armor forces and the emergence of Blitzkrieg combined arms operations – Soviet military theorists developed the concept of the military technical revolution. During the early phases of the Cold War, Soviet planners worried that the United States' dominance in the development of advanced military technologies – precision guided munitions, cruise missiles, and stealth technology – would undermine Soivet plans to overwhelm NATO forces with a mass of relatively less sophisticated forces. Their concern deepened after evaluating the success of the Israeli employment of precision-guided weapons against Soviet-designed weapon systems and tactics during the Yom Kippur War.[6] However, the Soviet's evaluation of the shift in the character of warfare was limited primarily to the American technological innovations,

---

[4] For additional references and works on the nature and theory of military revelation see: Jeremy Black, A Military Revolution? Military Change and European Society, 1550-1800; Andrew Krepievich, "Cavalry to Computer: The Pattern of Military Revolutions," Clifford J. Rogers, "The Military Revolution Debate, Readings on the Military Transformation of Early Modern Europe," and Crane Briton, *The Anatomy of the Military Transformation of Early Modern Europe.*

[5] Knox and Murray, *The Dynamics of Military Revolution, 1300-2050*, 1-2.

[6] Ibid., 3-4.

which caused them to focus on matching technological capability versus evaluating whether or not they needed to adjust their strategic or operational concepts.

Andrew W. Marshall, the long-serving director of the Pentagon's Office of Net Assessment, acknowledged the value of using the Soviet approach to evaluating historical and contemporary military operations to determine whether military-technical revolutions had indeed occurred that would necessitate fundamental adjustments in United States strategy.[7] Marshall and the Office of Net Assessment recognized that the Soviet analysis placed too much emphasis on technology and elected to replace the term "military-technical revolution" with "revolution in military affairs." The objective was an attempt to ensure that the analysis of potential military revolutions included the evaluation of changes in the strategic environment, strategy, and doctrine along with technology to determine the extent of potential changes in the future of warfare.[8]

Marshall was concerned that the United States seemed overly focused with reliance upon the promises of new technology to reduce the duration and cost of war, while minimizing the loss of life and overall destruction of enemy forces and infrastructure required to obtain decisive victory. The success of new technologies in the Gulf War spurred many military strategists and Pentagon programmers to advocate that a military revolution had occurred. The result was a justification of a dramatic shift of United States military procurement to costly high technology networked systems. However, the lack of a corresponding seismic change to society, strategy and military

---

[7] Ibid., 4.
[8] Ibid., 4.

13

organizations indicate that Marshall's concerns about overreliance on technological advances were deemed unwarranted by the Department of Defense.[9]

Many historians and scholars will incorrectly use the terms "military revolution" and "revolutions in military affairs" simultaneously. These two terms have very distinct meanings and have different levels of impact. Historians Williamson Murray and MacGregor Knox equate military revolutions to earthquakes due to their often uncontrollable, unpredictable, and unforeseeable characteristics that result in systemic changes in both politics and society. This results in "fundamental changes to the framework of war…recasting society and the state as well as military organizations."[10]

Military organizations will inevitably create new approaches to warfare that integrate the changes and advances caused by the systemic political and social changes of a military revolution. The resulting changes in military tactics, doctrine, and organization are less expansive revolutions in military affairs. Military analyst Andrew Krepinevich describes the process to identify that a revolution in military affairs has occurred:

> …the application of new technologies into a significant number of military systems combines with innovative operational concepts and organizational adaptations in a way that fundamentally alters the character and conduct of conflict. It does so by producing a dramatic increase—often an order of magnitude or greater—in the combat potential and military effectiveness of armed forces.[11]

During a period of military revolution, several changes in military affairs may occur to integrate the changes to the character of warfare within military organizations and doctrine. The cyber military revolution has indeed been an

---

[9] Ibid., 4.
[10] Bryon Greenwald, "Understanding Change: An Intellectual and Practical Study of Military Innovation-U.S. Army Antiaircraft Artillery and the Battle for Legitimacy, 1917-45" (PhD diss, Ohio State University, 2004)
[11] Ibid.

earthquake that has shaken the foundations of politics and society. There will be

several revolutions in military affairs as cyberspace continues to develop that will

be aftershocks large enough to continue to shake the foundations of military

tactics, doctrine, and organizations.

The Five Military Revolutions and their Key Attributes

Historians Knox and Murray theorize that only five periods in the past 400 years

of Western civilization have met the criteria for military revolutions by fundamentally

changing society, military strategy, and altering the course of warfare.

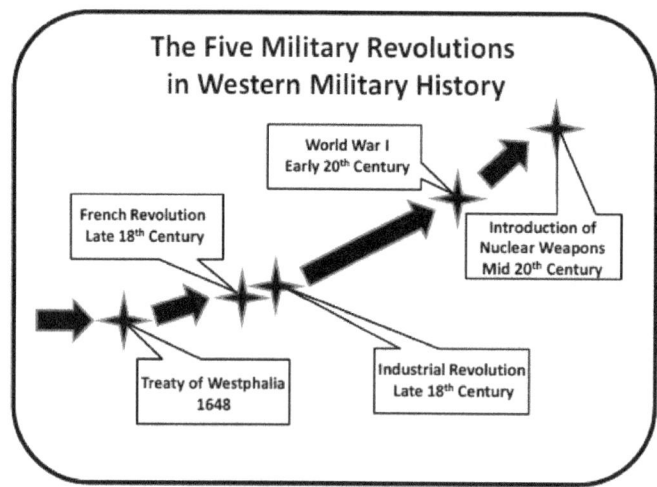

Figure 1.1: Military Revolutions in Western Military History[12]

A brief review of the periods in history identified in Figure 1.1 will illustrate that military

revolutions have occurred when there was a nexus of transformative changes in society

and military organizations. The review will describe the key attribute of each military

revolution (See figure 1.2). The additive nature of the key attributes is critical to

---

[12] Figure was developed by the author to provide a graphical depiction of the five recognized military revolutions by historians Williamson Murray and MacGregor Knox.

understanding the degree to which each military revolution has affected the course of warfare.

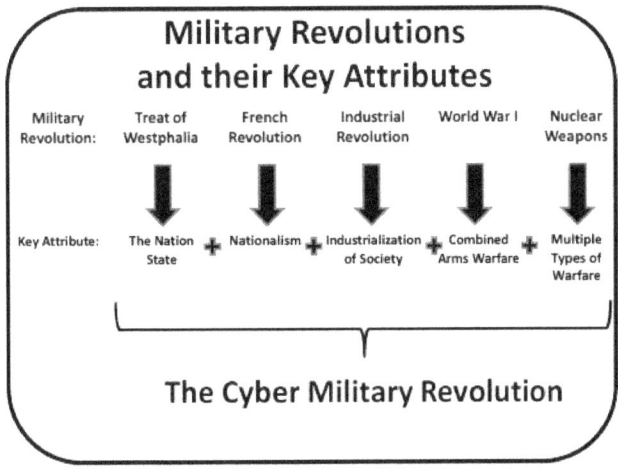

Figure 1.2 Military Revolutions and Their Key Attributes[13]

Following the review of each military revolution, an analysis of the current strategic environment or a specific cyber warfare case study will show that a new military revolution has occurred, why it is the most complex revolution to date, and that a comprehensive new framework of war will be required to address the multiple possible paths of future warfare.

The First Military Revolution and the Rise of the Nation-State

The genesis and basis for the first military revolution comes from the largest societal transformation in western history, the development of the nation-state in the 17th century. The growth of nation-states after the Treaty of Westphalia in 1648 spurred a corresponding transformation in the armed services. Before the rise of nation-states, wealthy monarchs or landowners waged war with feudal and mercenary armies that were

---

[13] Figure was developed by the author to illustrate the key attributes of each military revolution, how those attributes are additive to each other and their cumulative impact on successive revolutions.

limited in size based primarily upon the individual wealth of their royal or feudal lord. However, when the armies were not regularly paid, they often mutinied and pillaged the lands they had protected and defended.[14]

As warfare evolved and became more expensive, wealthier lords and kings bought out or forced out their less well off rivals and centralization of the state began. With the rise of monetized economics, central authorities began taxing land owners and enforcing their taxing authority by employing paid armies. Eventually, centralization and maintenance of power by and for the nation-state overrode other reasons to fight, often for religion, and by the mid-to-late 17th century, the European nation-state became a reality. As this revolution in power occurred, it led to the creation and maintenance of standing armies and navies—the key attribute of the first military revolution.[15] It also shifted the balance of power towards the nation-states that were able to maintain the societal and economic stability required to support and maintain a professional armed force, the key attribute of the first military revolution.

The evolution of the nation-state is also a cornerstone for the subsequent military revolutions. As one looks to cyber security in the 21st century, one must acknowledge that cyber security will require national wealth to support professional cyber forces, defend national cyber infrastructure, and develop and implement an effective cyber strategy. However, as the nation slowly centralizes its cyber security, strategists must be aware that the cyber military revolution has attributes that harkens back to the mercenary and feudal period preceding the rise of nation-states and professional fighting forces. The use of non-state hackers as "cyber mercenaries" to support a nation-state's goals and

---

[14] Knox and Murray, *The Dynamics of Military Revolution, 1300-2050*, 7.
[15] Ibid., 8.

objectives (or maraud on their own) increases the complexity of understanding the full impact of cyber on the future of warfare.

On December 27, 2008, Israel responded to hundreds of rocket attacks by Hamas and launched Operation CAST LEAD. The campaign started with a week of airstrikes by Israel against Hamas forces and infrastructure, followed by 18 days of ground operations.[16] Palestinian officials claimed Israeli actions caused over 1,000 deaths, massive property damage, and large amounts of civilian casualties. "This provoked outrage in the Arab and Muslim communities, which manifested itself in a spike of anti-Semitic incidents around the world, calls for violent attacks on Jewish interests worldwide, and cyber attacks on Israeli websites."[17]

Lacking the financial ability to fund a professional army to counter Israeli air and ground operations, or produce an independent cyber capability, Hamas employed and supported hackers as "cyber mercenaries" to attack Israel. Post-conflict analysis determined that hackers were able to participate virtually in the battle from the comfort of their homes or Internet cafes in Morocco, Algeria, Saudi Arabia, Turkey, and the Palestinian territories.[18]

Instead of attacking the Israeli government or military systems directly with high-profile cyber attacks in an attempt to degrade Israeli combat operations, the hackers conducted indirect attacks and plundered the websites and servers of thousands of Israeli businesses and banks. The hackers' objective was to coerce Israel to cease their combat operations by disrupting the Israeli economy and sabotaging strategic communications.

[16] Global Security, "Operation Cast Lead," Global Security.org, http://www.globalsecurity.org/military/world/war/operation-cast-lead.htm (accessed November 29, 2011).
[17] Jeffrey Carr, *Inside Cyber Warfare* (Sebastopol, CA: O'Reilly Media, 2010), 19.
[18] Ibid., 19.

Economically, the hackers focused their attacks on the websites and servers at Israeli businesses and banks websites and servers with the goal of inflicting millions of dollars in losses through their inability to complete on-line transactions and the need to invest in increased computer security systems.[19]

The hackers also used cyber technology effectively to advance the external perception of Hamas and increase support for its cause. In an attempt to influence the Israeli people and businesses now suffering direct financial damage because of Israeli combat operations, they left messages on thousands of websites that stated the cyber attacks would stop once Israel ceased combat operations and immediately withdrew their forces from Gaza.[20] Additionally, the hackers looked to increase the size of the ranks by linking their actions to fulfilling the Muslim religious obligation of Jihad:

> Use [the hacking skills] God has given you as bullets in the face of the Jewish Zionists. We cannot fight them with our bodies, but we can fight them with our minds and hands…. By God this is Jihad.[21]

A key attribute or outcome of the first military revolution was the nation-state's ability to raise a professional armed force. The size and strength of a nation's armed forces and the ability to project power or win battles was dependent on the economic strength of the country. However, as the cyber response to Operation CAST LEAD shows, the use of mercenary hackers in the cyber domain has the potential to alter this traditional relationship and helps to illustrate the increased complexity of the cyber military revolution. A less powerful nation can now utilize a significantly cheaper "cyber mercenary" force instead of developing its own suite of independent traditional

---

[19] Ibid., 19.
[20] Ibid., 22.
[21] Ibid., 22.

conventional capabilities as a method to project power effectively or to coerce a more

developed nation-state to change its course.

The Second Military Revolution and the Impact of Nationalism

The next major vector change in the conduct of warfare was a result of a

significant shift in society that occurred during the French Revolution. French leaders

were able to institute a levee en masse and exponentially expand the size of their army by

stoking the flames of nationalism and calling citizens to serve higher calling for the

greater good of the nation.[22] Carl von Clausewitz accurately summarized the significant

change this would have on the framework of warfare:

> Suddenly war again became the business of the people – a people
> of thirty million, all of whom considered themselves to be
> citizens... The people became a participant in war; instead of
> governments and armies as heretofore, the full weight of the nation
> was thrown into the balance. The resources and efforts now
> available for use surpassed all conventional limits; nothing new
> inhibited the vigor with which war could be waged, and
> consequently the opponents of France faced the utmost peril.[23]

The peril the opponents of France faced is an example of the potential cost of

failing to recognize a military revolution and responding with the timely adjustment to

one's national strategy as necessary, based upon the scale of changes to the strategic

environment. Numerous battlefield defeats was the cost many nations had to bear until

they could mobilize their populace and build their armies to the size required to defeat

France.[24]

The merging of politics and warfare through nationalism is the key element of the

second military revolution and is a critical component of subsequent military revolutions.

---

[22] Knox and Murray, *The Dynamics of Military Revolution, 1300-2050*, 8.

[23] Carl von Clausewitz, *On War*, eds. and trans. Michael Howard and Peter Paret (Princeton: Princeton University Press, 1976), 592.

[24] Knox and Murray, *The Dynamics of Military Revolution, 1300-2050*, 8-9.

The ability to use the cyber domain to stoke the flames of Egyptian nationalism in April of 2008 foreshadowed the impact the cyber military revolution and nationalistic zeal would have on the Arab Spring and on the future of warfare.

On 6 April, 2008, textile workers decided to strike at political corruption within the industry as state-run companies were "privatized" in what was seen as very corrupt deals. Although, the government had promised privatization would improve worker conditions, economic conditions and wages did not advance. Historically, these types of strikes would draw several hundred protestors. In contrast, after Internet activists decided to support the strike and establish a Facebook page, over 70,000 individuals joined the effort, causing the government to take notice. The Egyptian government established a new security force division dedicated to "policing" the Internet. They also employed their own hackers to spread pro-government propaganda on websites, blogs, and social networks. The threat of security force detainment and interrogation eventually curtailed the growth of participation in this case. However, it highlighted the degree to which the cyber domain can be a powerful shifting force in politics. It also demonstrated the ability of the state to orchestrate, control, or limit the movements of nationalism in the cyber age may be increasingly difficult.[25]

These type of events also show the complexity of developing a successful framework of war that can address the ability for cyber attackers to jump from one "front" to another in the cyber domain. A cyber attack may start as a criminal act, but potential adversaries can utilize the same tactics, techniques and procedures to escalate the attacks to a level of cyber-terrorism or direct attacks that can cripple a nation's

---

[25] Wael Ghonim, *Revolution 2.0 The Power of the People is Great than The People in Power: A Memoir,* (New York: Houghton Mifflin Harcourt, 2012), 35-36.

infrastructure. Many nations use different organizations or government departments to defend against cyber crimes, terrorism, and direct attacks on military or private computer infrastructure. Cyber attackers can easily exploit the seams between these organizations and transition the scope or purpose of attack without any significant change to their methods.

In early January 2012, an incident that started as an apparent act of cyber crime escalated into full cyber warfare between multiple hacker groups from Israel, Saudi Arabia and the United Arab Emirates. Both sides in this struggle attempted to justify their actions through nationalism and independent acts of cyber deterrence for their individual nations.

On January 3, 2012, a hacker group identified as Group XP from Saudi Arabia, claimed to have stolen credit card information from over 400,000 Israelis. Three major Israeli banks confirmed that their systems were successfully penetrated and that they had taken action to prevent misuse of the compromised credit cards; however, they claimed only 15,000 accounts were affected. The day after the Israeli banks reported the incident was not as large as Group XP claimed; the hackers released the information on another 11,000 accounts and threatened to release the details from 60,000 additional cardholders.[26]

The first Israeli response to the cyber crime attacks did not come from the government, but rather an Israeli college student, Amr Phadida. In only eight hours, Phadida was able to analyze the attacks and track the identity of the lead Group XP

[26] The Next Web, "Middle East, Part of the Next Web Family," The Next Web, http://thenextweb.com/me/2012/01/18/everything-you-need-to-know-about-the-ongoing-israeli-saudi-hacker-struggle/ (accessed January 23, 2012).

hacker to a 19-year-old United Arab Emirates citizen currently living in Mexico.[27]

Phadida acted on his own initiative to investigate and provide information his

government could use in their investigation and to attempt to stop or degrade Group XPs

efforts.

On January 8, 2012, the Israeli Foreign Minister, Danny Ayalon acknowledged

the attacks and elevated their seriousness by classifying them as acts of cyber-terrorism

and breaches of Israeli sovereignty:

> We will take firm action against those who compromise our
> security including through cyber-terrorism, and if necessary we
> will use international law enforcement. Cyber-terrorism is the new
> battleground and just as we defeated our opponents on every other
> field...we will defeat this as well.[28]

While tacitly admitting that Israel did not have a defense for this attack, he also

tried to smother independent acts of support from the Israeli populace that already

possessed the skills necessary to defend or deter Israel's adversaries in the cyber domain:

> We call on Israeli citizens to abide by (the law). Just as the Israeli
> government has found answers for terrorism, we will find answers
> to this challenge...we call on Israeli citizens not to...act as
> vigilantes.[29]

Conversely, a Hamas representative recognized the value of fanning the flames of Pan

Arab nationalism to increase support for Group XP and solicit participation for additional

efforts in an attempt to extend the damage beyond the Israeli banking system. Hamas

also recognized and promoted that hackers, motivated by national zeal, could use the

cyber domain to inflict significant economic and psychological damages on Israel:

> We, in Hamas, bless this effort and urge the Arab youth to activate
> and develop it; we consider that this effort has the same value as

---

[27] Ibid.
[28] Ibid.
[29] Ibid.

any kind of resistance means used by the Palestinian young men in the land of Palestine. We stress our solidarity with the Arab hackers in the face of the Zionist threats and call upon the Arab youth not to pay any attention to these cowardly threats and to use all possible means through the virtual space to confront the Zionist crimes.[30]

An Israeli hacker that identified himself as 0xOmer chose to ignore his foreign minister's appeals to stay out of the cyber-skirmish and on January 11, 2012, announced a successful cyber attack against multiple Arab banks in the Middle East that resulted in the compromise of over 50,000 credit card accounts. 0xOmer designed his actions to serve as a deterrent for future Arab actions against Israeli interests and encouraged Israeli hackers to respond to any additional Arab attacks with actions of similar or greater scope and impact. The deterrence strategy failed, and over the next several days, both sides threatened and then released additional credit card and account information.[31]

On January 13, 2012, another Israeli hacker named "Hannibal" entered the virtual battle by claiming to have stolen 30 million Arab Facebook and email user accounts and passwords and threatened to destroy their online experience. He also took the Israeli Foreign Minister to task for not enlisting the aid of hackers supportive of Israel to join the cause in protecting Israel and attacking Arab systems. Hannibal later escalated his efforts and published another post attempting to deter further action against Israeli systems by threatening to cause billions of dollars in damages by publishing account information from 10 million Saudi and Iranian bank accounts.[32]

The deterrent strategy failed again and an increasing numbers of Saudi hackers combined to strengthen their attack efforts. Showing how quickly and easily cyber

---

[30] Ibid.
[31] Ibid.
[32] Ibid.

attacks can escalate from acts of crime to terrorism to a direct assault on a nation's economy, a small number of Saudi hackers were able to bring down the websites of the Israeli airline, El Al, and the Tel Aviv Stock Exchange.[33] The hackers again linked their efforts to the Arab national objectives and stated that they would decrease the intensity of their efforts if the Israeli Foreign Minister apologized for his statements and Israel reversed their direction and efforts to counter cyber attacks.[34]

The Israeli response to the direct attack on their nation's economy was again limited to the hacker community. A group of Israeli hackers not affiliated with the Israeli government took on the self-appointed mantel of the "IDF-Team" and attacked, then took down, the official stock exchange websites in Saudi Arabia and the United Arab Emirates. After another few rounds of exchanging cyber attacks, additional hacker groups joined the IDF-Team and issued a statement that sounded as if they were establishing Israeli national cyber policy:

> We won't attack for no reason. We are waiting to see if there are more attacks on Israel. Our next steps will be taken slowly...the message we wish to pass is that we are not frightened to retaliate and we won't be frightened on continuing with the attacks.[35]

Burgeoning nationalism raised the size of armies in the early industrial age and is having similar effects in the "age of cyber." The actions of the Israeli and Arab hackers demonstrate that cyber technology offers a battlefield with an ease of entry and one for which individual nation-states may be unable to provide a barrier for control. Individuals or groups of individuals can act in support of what they perceive to be their national interests regardless of whether or not they have the formal or even informal

---

[33] Ibid.
[34] Ibid.
[35] Ibid.

support of the nation-state. These factors will complicate the development and employment of a successful cyber framework robust enough to address the influence of nationalism in support of an increasing range of cyber attacks from crime, terrorism, or direct support of military operations in the physical domains.

The Third Military Revolution and the Rise of the Machines

The Industrial Revolution that began in Britain in the late 18th century radically transformed western society from a rural agrarian culture to an urban, industrialized society and irrevocably changed the conduct of warfare. Industrialization provided Britain with tremendous wealth and the ability to counter the French numerical advantage born out of nationalism. More importantly, it highlights how seismic societal and economic shifts can alter the framework of warfare even before new technologies developed for civilian use migrate to the battlefield. As Knox and Murray highlight, the Industrial Revolution's impact on the Napoleonic Wars was more indirect. Industrial technology offered the armed forces no major battlefield innovations until the mid-nineteenth century; the British Army under Wellington fought in thoroughly traditional fashion.

> Yet behind the scenes, the Industrial Revolution nevertheless provided the British government with the enormous wealth needed to cobble together and sustain the great coalitions that eventually defeated Napoleon. The alliance of 1813 that brought together Britain, Austria, Russia, and Prussia at last mobilized the continent's resources sufficiently to overwhelm Napoleon's tactical-operational genius. Britain's financial power was the decisive force behind that mobilization.[36]

Similar to the Industrial Revolution, the cyber military revolution has greatly reshaped multiple aspects of society. The development of the cyber infrastructure to

---

[36] Knox and Murray, *The Dynamics of Military Revolution, 1300-2050*, 9.

support the growth of the World Wide Web and the rapid expansion of social media is changing the way society communicates, conducts business, and even wages war. However, the focus of the cyber military revolution often tends to be on the attempts to use cyber technology to defeat, degrade or deny an adversary's ability to use their computer networks and infrastructure. This focus is far too narrow. Regular use of social media innovations are a major subcomponent of the cyber military revolution and are integral to understanding the ongoing fundamental reshaping of society and how it will affect the future of warfare.

Web services such as Facebook, Twitter, YouTube, texting, and political blogs are in fact weapons of cyber warfare that have already had tremendous battlefield effects even before they are partially militarized. The inability of the Tunisian and Egyptian governments to foresee and understand the development, pace, and the ultimate revolutionary impact of cyber and social media was a prominent factor in their downfall. At a 2011 cyber security conference in Abu Dubai, Michael Hayden, former Director of the Central Intelligence Agency and the National Security Agency, described the power of the cyber military revolution by outlining how quickly social media was able to triumph over three decades of repression of political dissent and free speech in Egypt:

> Omar Suleman [the former head of the Egyptian intelligence service] was a very good intelligence officer... [He] was so good at his job that he was able to keep Mubarak in power against all opposition for more than three decades. And yet, the immolation of a fruit merchant in a small Tunisian city set in motion a revolution enabled by the cyber world, enabled by social media. A few weeks later there were a million people in Tahrir Square in Cairo, calling for the overthrow of the Egyptian government. In other words, all of Omar's skills he used to maintain support for

Mubarak were insufficient to meet the volume, and the velocity of what was coming at him enabled by this domain.[37]

The fall of the Tunisian and Egyptian governments serve as an example of what can happen when restrictive governments fail to recognize that a military revolution has occurred and how the shift in society caused by cyber and social networks was enough to upend the status quo. In many repressive Arab nations, the ability of the populace to voice their opinions freely or attempt to hold their governments accountable for what individuals or groups perceive as unjust actions or policies has been severely limited. Historically, governments were able to keep a very tight rein on information availability and public dissemination. Social media is a key component of the cyber military revolution and it has changed the entire information paradigm.

The original intent of social media was to provide Internet users a means to inform, entertain, and create communities of common interest. However, it did not take long for many of those Internet users to recognize the potential of social media to mobilize support for a cause, provide command and control over a movement or demonstration, and offer an anonymous method to hold governments accountable.[38] The independent social media will continue to have significant regional impacts, with the estimated expansion of Internet users in the Arab world alone growing from an estimated 40 million current users to over 100 million by 2015.[39] This expansion in the social media user-base and supporting cyber infrastructure is far outpacing authoritarian regimes' ability to counter or repress the efforts. Before the downfall of the Mubarak

---

[37] Knowledge@Wharton, "In the Middle East, Cyberattacks are Flavored with Political Rhetoric," Knowledge@Wharton, http://knowledge.wharton.upeen.edu/arabic/article.cfm?articleid=2774 (accessed January 23, 2012).

[38] Jeff Ghannam, "Social Media in the Arab World: Leading up to the Uprisings of 2011," Center for International Media Assistance, http://cima.ned.org/sites/default/files/CIMA-Arab_Social_Media-Report%20-%2010-25-11.pdf (accessed January 17, 2012).

[39] Ibid.

regime, the Egyptian interior ministry attempted and failed to monitor the Facebook activity of over 5 million Egyptian users while looking for signs of political opposition and social activism. As Facebook collaboration has now expanded to over 17 million users in the Middle East region, repressive governments are realizing they can no longer maintain, control, or curtail anti-government collaboration and the exchange of information from inside and outside their borders.[40]

Sami Ben Gharbia, a leading Tunisian dissident blogger and Director of Global Voice Advocacy, outlined how protestors used social media to promote their strategic communications and directly influenced what appeared on the traditional media outlets around the world. Tunisian protestors would collaborate on Facebook to develop the theme or message they wanted to promote. They then would post updates and links to videos on Twitter for international media monitoring the Arab Spring:

> We rely on a network of activists from around the Arab world in the first instance. And those activists, from Mauritania to Iraq, they know each other. They are training each other on how to download video, how to use Google maps. These reports can be translated into multiple languages and resent for media around the world. That was the echo chamber of the struggle on the street.[41]

These actions demonstrate how cyber and social media are regional coordination tools that have the ability to produce global strategic effects. The ability to provide significant assistance in effecting a regime change without firing a bullet demonstrates the current and future potential that the use of social media can have on the character of warfare. Tunisian dissidents are promoting the revolutionary capabilities of cyber technology and have shared their social media tactics, techniques, and procedures with

---

[40] Ibid.
[41] Ibid.

others engaging in similar efforts. Protests in Lebanon, Jordan, Yemen, and Syria bear the marks of the Tunisian efforts.[42]

The Fourth Military Revolution and the Beginnings of Combined Arms Warfare

The First World War is the clearest example of the additive nature of military revolutions. The militarization of industrial developments designed for civil use, such as railroads, steamships, and the telegraph, started in the United States Civil War and then came of age in World War I.[43] These technologies provided unprecedented mobility, the capability to command and control an army over vast distances, and the ability to project combat power routinely over the high seas. More importantly, the fusion of fully developed nation-state centralization of fiscal and foreign policy, rampant nationalism, and the militarization of new technologies via robust industrial economies dramatically altered the scope and scale of warfare. Cumulatively, armies now had the destructive combat power to inflict incredible amounts of casualties, all supported by a nationalistic zeal that provided a constant stream of manpower to feed a deadly, stagnant war of attrition.

After World War I, in reaction to this enormous bloodletting, military theorists on all sides tried to invent ways to restore mobility to warfare. Of all the warring nations, the Germans were the most effective at creating a warfighting doctrine that harnessed emerging technologies (armor, mechanization, aviation, and wireless signal), intelligent maneuver doctrine, personal leadership, and fanatical nationalistic zeal. At its core, the Blitzkrieg doctrine leveraged these new technologies in a fashion that combined all arms

---

[42] Ibid.
[43] Knox and Murray, *The Dynamics of Military Revolution, 1300-2050*, 9.

(armor, infantry, artillery, and airpower) in a synergistic fashion to disrupt and destroy more pedantic and defensively focused militaries.

Like the marriage of armor, infantry, artillery, and airpower into a integrated and powerful force, the cyber military revolution also bears the marks of the successful militarization and integration of cyber innovations to redefine combined arms warfare by fusing attacks in the physical domain with supporting actions or attacks in the cyber domain. Maturing cyber capabilities significantly increase the complexity of warfare as more nations, organizations, and individuals recognize its power to provide instantaneous virtual worldwide mobility, its ability to develop a global command and control system using simple communication tools, and its capacity to project power or influence at the speed of light. As the following case study illustrates, nations will require a strategy that can effectively deter or counter attacks on the physical battlefield that are more easily identified and may be accompanied by simultaneous attacks on the virtual battlefield that are increasingly difficult to detect, deter, and defeat.

On September 6, 2007, Israeli F-15s and F-16s took off on a supposed training mission over the Mediterranean Sea. Minutes after launching, the aircraft turned east, neutralized a coastal Syrian radar station, and then flew undetected for eighteen minutes through Syrian airspace before attacking a suspected undeclared Syrian nuclear reactor next to the Euphrates River, seventy-five miles south of the Turkish and Syrian border.[44]

Bomb damage assessment of the target area indicated that Operation ORCHARD was a complete conventional success. Israeli commandos had penetrated Syrian territory and provided the precise laser targeting necessary for the formation of seven Israeli

---

[44] Erich Follath and Holger Stark, "The Story of Operation Orchard," Spiegel, http://www.spiegel.de/international/world/0,1518,658663,00.html (accessed December 2, 2011).

Boeing F-15Is to engage and eliminate the nuclear weapons facility successfully with only one surgical strike.

Despite the destruction of the Syrian coastal air defense radar site, the Israeli non-stealthy F-15s and F-16s should not have been able to penetrate so far into Syrian airspace without detection. On the night of the raid, the Syrians had a fully operational Russian-built air defense system with networked early warning and target tracking radars along with mobile tactical SAM systems that provided more than enough capability to detect and defeat fourth generation fighter aircraft such as the F-15 and F-16.[45]

Syria demanded answers from the Russian government regarding the technology that blinded their ground-based air defense systems and controllers during the attack and what allowed it to occur. While Russian contractors desperately looked for an implementation or user error to prevent prospective buyers of their air defense systems from abandoning sales that were on the negotiation table, computer experts around the world offered the plausible explanation for the Israeli success: cyber warfare.[46] There were initially several explanations for how the Israelis used cyber warfare to support the attack, but over time, two primary theories have emerged as the most likely methods used by the Israelis. The first theory is that the Israelis used a low observable unmanned aerial vehicle (UAV) that utilized a technology similar to the U.S. developed "Suter" airborne network attack system. This type of technology locates and penetrates enemy sensors

---

[45]David A. Fulghum, "Why Syria's Air Defense Systems Failed to Detect Israelis." Aviation Week, http://www.aviationweek.com/aw/blogs/defense/index.jsp?plckController=Blog&plckBlogPage=BlogView Post&newspaperUserId=27ec4a53-dcc8-42d0-bd3a-01329aef79a7&plckPostId=Blog%3a27ec4a53-dcc8-42d0-bd3a-01329aef79a7Post%3a2710d024-5eda-416c-b117-ae6d649146cd&plckScript=blogScript&plckElementId=blogDest (accessed December 2, 2011).

[46] Clark and Knake, *Cyber War*, 6.

and supporting systems, then manipulates connecting data streams to present false or misleading images.[47]

The second leading theory is that the Israelis penetrated the Russian computer code that integrates the Syrian air defense system and installed a "trapdoor" that would allow external control and manipulation during the duration of the raid, or upon activation would use a pre-programmed injected code to autonomously present false data on the screens of the air defense operators.[48]

In either case, the Israeli ability to use the cyber domain to mislead and to neutralize the Syrian air defense system enabled a very successful conventional attack. The cyber military revolution will allow nations or armed forces to use similar expanded combined arms methods that fuse actions in the virtual cyber domain with actions in the physical domains of land, sea, air and space. The United States must recognize that the cyber military revolution offers less developed nations or adversaries the possibility of a cost-effective means to neutralize, degrade or defeat superior technology in order to permit the effective employment of less advanced, more conventional attack systems or methods.

The Fifth Military Revolution; Nuclear Weapons Change Everything

The impact of the two atomic explosions that ended the Second World War went far beyond the island of Japan. The development and use of nuclear weapons was a paradigm shattering military revolution. The incredible destructive power of nuclear technology fundamentally shaped the national strategy of the United States and molded

---

[47] Aviation Week. "Israeli used Electronic Attack in Air Strike against Syrian Mystery Target." Aviation Week. http://www.aviationweek.com/aw/generic/story_generic.jsp?channel=awst&id=news/aw100807p2.xml (accessed December 2, 2011).
    [48] Ibid.

the way America thought it would fight for decades to come. The prevailing United States' concept of post-World War II strategy was to utilize its initial monopoly of nuclear weapons and delivery capability as a deterrent to counter the growing threat of the Soviet Union.[49]

Several factors contributed to the transformation of the American warfighting strategy based upon nuclear forces and capability. The military revolutions prior to the development of atomic weapons demonstrated the incredible amount of manpower and resources required to achieve the equivalent destructive potential and effects of nuclear weapons. Nations needed to mobilize their entire societies and retool and refocus industry for nearly exclusive support to the war effort. These efforts were necessary to generate the combat power required by large armies, multi-ocean navies, and expanding air forces to defeat enemy forces around the globe. Nuclear weapons, and the ability to deliver them, gave United States national leaders a capability to influence other nations to do America's will without the necessary investment required to maintain the equivalent capability in conventional combat power and might possibly prevent the need to fight at all.

The threat of the Soviet Union and its support for the expansion of communism were anomalies to American traditional post-war paradigms and required adjustments to its post-war strategies. The challenge facing President Truman was his desire to continue New Deal social programs, refocus American industry to civilian applications, and maintain a credible defensive strategy that would confront the growing Soviet threat. The United States needed a strategy that would contain Soviet expansionism, but not break the bank.

---

[49]David W. Tarr, *American Strategy in the Nuclear Age*, (New York: Macmillan, 1966), 69.

The United States' monopoly on nuclear weapons and the ability to deliver them would not last forever. As the Soviets and Chinese gained nuclear technology, America's increased reliance on the deterrent value of nuclear weapons proved insufficient.

Eisenhower recognized the approaching loss of advantage in the nuclear arena and shifted national policy within his New Look strategy that combined massive retaliation with collective defense and covert action to give the United States more options when responding to Soviet expansionism. However, the main shortcomings in shifting the paradigm of our national strategy towards a nuclear response focus were Korea and Vietnam. [50]

The Soviet Union and China supported the expansion of communism into Korea and Vietnam, but successive United States presidents were unwilling to utilize nuclear weapons as a response to these conflicts. During the years leading up to Korea and Vietnam, the United States' focus and investment was on developing the strategy and forces that would harness the power of the nuclear military revolution. The growth of the Strategic Air Command, super carriers to support navy aircraft capable of nuclear weapons delivery, and the pentomic army structure are examples of the manner by which all military services shifted their acquisition, organizational structure, doctrine, and strategy to support fighting with a nuclear force. [51] Although this investment might help in countering the numerical advantage the Soviets would have in another war on the European continent, it ultimately led to an unbalanced force that was not capable of

---

[50] Tarr, *American Strategy in the Nuclear Age*, 69-75.
[51] A.J. Bacevich, The Pentomic ERA: The US Army Between Korea and Vietnam, (Washington DC, NDU Press, 1986), 105-109.

giving national leaders a sufficient range of options outside a nuclear response. President

Kennedy recognized this and called for a shift in national strategy to flexible response.[52]

The Cyber Military Revolution; Everything is Changing Again

Flexible response is the underlying foundation of our current joint doctrine.

Recently, President Obama reinforced this lesson from the Cold War when he warned of

re-building our armed forces based on a narrow strategy that limits our capability to fight

across the full spectrum of conflict. He also highlighted the significance of

understanding the role of cyber in the future of warfare in order to ensure that the United

States has the capability to respond across the new expanded and complex full spectrum

of operations:

> Going forward, we will also remember the lessons of history and
> avoid repeating the mistakes of the past when our military was left
> ill-prepared for the future. As we end today's wars and reshape
> our Armed Forces, we will ensure that our military is agile,
> flexible, and ready for the full range of contingencies. In
> particular, we will continue to invest in the capabilities critical to
> future success, including intelligence, surveillance, and
> reconnaissance; counterterrorism; countering weapons of mass
> destruction; operating in anti-access environments; and prevailing
> in all domains, including cyber.[53]

In the age of cyber technology, the United States must be prepared to respond

along the entire expanded range of military conflict. The challenge facing senior leaders

today is the same that President Truman faced following World War II. Similar to the

introduction of nuclear weapons, the cyber military revolution has presented national

leaders with an increasingly powerful weapon that can deter or devastate an adversary's

information systems, economy, and even physical infrastructure—all without directly

---

[52] Tarr, *American Strategy in the Nuclear Age*, 98-101.
[53] U.S. Department of Defense. *Sustaining U.S. Global Leadership: Priorities for 21st Century Defense.* (Washington DC: Department of Defense, 5 January 2012), Cover Letter.

killing anyone! In a period of intense budget constraint and a desire to increase domestic spending to spur job creation, there will be calls to base the foundation of our warfighting strategy on a military revolution defined by a singular technology. Some will cite the success of the Stuxnet cyber attack, a form of malware specifically designed to attack the industrial control systems of nuclear power plants, as a case study that demonstrates the cyber military revolution has provided a more cost-effective and less risky method to project power in the "age of cyber".[54] A simple thumb drive and lines of computer code served as a weapon that caused physical damage to Iranian nuclear facilities and may have set back their nuclear weapons development program by years. However, the Stuxnet case study also highlights the complexities and challenges of this latest military revolution and the inherent danger and lack of response flexibility if our future warfighting strategies overemphasize or rely too heavily on cyber technology and capabilities.

In late September 2010, the Iranian government acknowledged that the Stuxnet computer virus had infected the IP addresses of over 30,000 industrial computer systems that control the critical operations in its nuclear development facilities.[55] Later, in November 2012, Iranian President Mahmoud Ahmadinejad admitted Stuxnet had caused physical damage to several of Iran's uranium enrichment centrifuges and put a temporary stop to Iran's nuclear fuel enrichment processes.[56] The Stuxnet computer virus is

---

[54] Yaakov Katz, "Stuxnet virus set back Iran's nuclear program by 2 years," Jerusalem ost, http://www.jpost.com/IranianThreat/News/Article.aspx?id=199475 (accessed January 29, 2012).

[55] Congressional Research Service, The *Stuxnet Computer Worm: Harbinger of an Emerging Warfare Capability*, December 2010 (Washington DC: Government Printing Officer, 2010), 3.

[56] Mark Clayton, "Stuxnet: Ahmadinejad admits cyberweapon hit Iran nuclear program," Christian Science Monitor, http://www.csmonitor.com/USA/2010/1130/Stuxnet-Ahmadinejad-admits-cyberweapon-hit-Iran-nuclear-program, (accessed 29 January 2012).

representative of the growing capability and potential impact of a cyber attack on a nation's critical infrastructure:

> Depending on the severity of the attack, the interconnected nature of the affected critical infrastructure facilities, and government preparation and response plans, entities and individuals relying on these facilities could be without life-sustaining or comforting services for a long period of time. The resulting damage to the nation's critical infrastructure could threaten many aspects of life, including the government's ability to safeguard national security interests.[57]

A cyber attack that demonstrates a known adversary's ability to degrade significantly or to render critical infrastructure systems inoperative has the potential of coercing a nation to bend or completely change its will. If a nation lacks the ability to defend against this type of attack, it is in a similar situation to nations that did not have the ability to respond to the threat of American nuclear attack when it was the sole nuclear power. However, Stuxnet also shows why the time gap between the have and have-nots of this type of destructive computer power will not exist for as long as it took other nations to match the United States in nuclear capabilities.

Although the Stuxnet computer code is very complex, it is available for download on the Internet with a description of its capabilities, a list of what systems it can effect, and the web addresses of supervisory control and data acquisition (SCADA) systems that are unsecured and vulnerable to attack. The ease of availability of this type of destructive

---

[57] Congressional Research Service, The *Stuxnet Computer Worm: Harbinger of an Emerging Warfare Capability*, December 2010 (Washington DC: Government Printing Officer, 2010), Executive Summary.

malware will allow nations, terrorists, and even super-empowered organizations or individuals to enter into this developing "cyber arms race" at a relatively low cost.[58]

In another example of the cyber military revolution's return to the use of mercenary forces, organizations have already discovered it is not necessary to have a cyber force or the independent ability to launch a malware attack. Nation-states and even cyber crime organizations have discovered it is less costly and easier to contract professional cyber forces or even rent time on already established networks of infected computers to accomplish their objectives. It is most likely just a matter of time before almost anyone can purchase a precision guided cybermuntion to conduct malicious acts against nations, groups, or even individuals. [59]

The ability to acquire cyber attack capability, combined with the growing aptitude for any adversary to use this type of attack without attribution, adds additional complexity to dealing with the challenges of the cyber military revolution. To date, no country or group has claimed responsibility for or has been exposed as the source of the Stuxnet attack. Leading experts in the cyber warfare and security field estimate that Stuxnet's complex 15,000 lines of code would take years and the resources of a wealthy nation(s) in order to support the necessary development, engineering, and controlled testing required to develop malware with such precise targeting capabilities.[60] While countries such as the United States, Israel, France, China and Russia may have the wealth and cyber expertise to develop cyber weapons as sophisticated at Stuxnet, the deterrent

---

[58] Congressional Research Service, The *Stuxnet Computer Worm: Harbinger of an Emerging Warfare Capability*, December 2010 (Washington DC: Government Printing Officer, 2010), Executive Summary.

[59] Ibid.

[60] Yaakov Katz, "Stuxnet virus set back Iran's nuclear program by 2 years," Jerusalem Post, http://www.jpost.com/IranianThreat/News/Article.aspx?id=199475 (accessed January 29, 2012).

value of massive retaliation through cyber attacks of Stuxnet's scale or larger is shrinking

every day. Less developed and wealthy nations can utilize similar and less complex

malware as a viable response option to cyber attacks of a larger scale, thus deterring a

more powerful nation from fully exploiting their cyber advantage.

The key attribute of both the nuclear weapon and cyber military revolutions is the

splintering effect they have had on the course of warfare. Starting with the nuclear

weapons revolution, Figure 1.4 outlines the four divergent vectors in the course of

warfare that occurred once the Soviet Union achieved nuclear parity with the United

States and the strategy of massive retaliation was no longer a valid option.

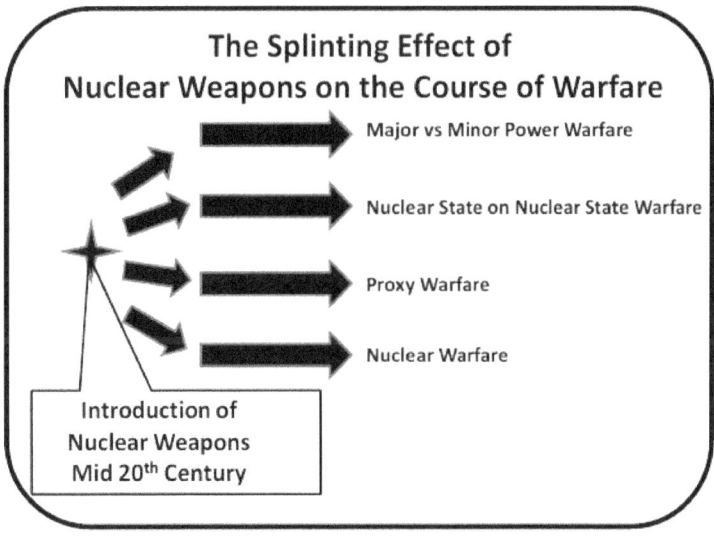

Figure 1.4 The Splintering Effect of Nuclear Weapons on the Course of Warfare[61]

The advent of nuclear weapons had a limiting effect on the possibility of state-on-state

warfare between the superpowers and their respective alliances. The destructive power

---

[61] This figure was developed by the author to illustrate the fracturing effect the introduction of nuclear weapons had, and how it generated multiple possible vectors the future of warfare could take.

of nuclear weapons essentially kept the Cold War cold.[62]   Even during periods of significantly heightened tensions, such as the Cuban Missile Crisis, the fear of crossing the nuclear threshold kept both sides from allowing the situation to escalate to armed conflict.

The ability to fight and attempt to win a nuclear war against another nuclear power became a path to mutually assured destruction, not a viable option. Although state-on-state conflict between the superpowers and nuclear war were possible paths of warfare that required maintaining the appropriate weapons and strategies to conduct those conflicts, limited proxy wars became the primary course of warfare during the era of bi-polar superpowers. The United States failed to anticipate the necessary adjustments to fight along this most likely path and resisted shifting strategy, organizations and doctrine from potential conflict with Soviets on the fields of Europe to the mountains of Korea, and jungles of Vietnam. It is a lesson the United States cannot repeat when determining how to address the multiple vectors the conduct of war can take with the introduction of the cyber domain.

Figure 1.5 shows that cyber technology has also opened the course of warfare to multiple divergent paths. However, unlike the paths created by the advent of nuclear weapons, each of the possible vectors is already occurring with equal frequency.

---

[62] Knox and Murray, *The Dynamics of Military Revolution, 1300-2050*, 4.

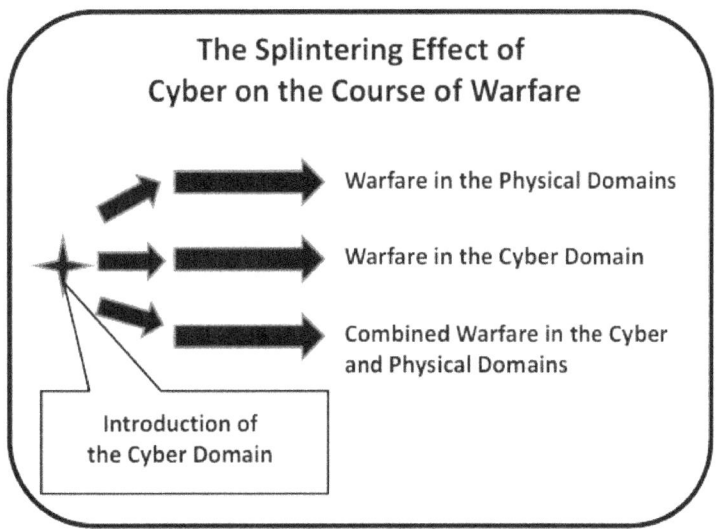

Figure 1.5 The Splintering Effect of Cyber on the Course of Warfare[63]

The fall of the Soviet Union reduced the threat of direct confrontation between superpowers and state-on-state conflict in the physical domains became a viable vector for the United States. Desert Storm, Kosovo, Iraq, and Afghanistan are all examples of the United States' willingness to enter unrestrained conventional conflict without having to worry about limitations caused by the possibility of escalation to the nuclear threshold.

Expanded combined arms warfare from the cyber and physical domains has been battle-tested and is likely to see increased use in future military operations and campaigns. The successful Israeli attack on the suspected Syrian nuclear facility is an example of integration of the cyber domain into conventional operations in the physical domain. The United States must ensure that it has a framework of war that can support a strategy that is able to meet diverse and complex attacks occurring in and from the virtual and physical domains simultaneously. Currently it does not.

---

[63] This figure was created by the author to demonstrate how the introduction of the cyber domain was a military revolution that also produced multiple possible paths warfare could take in the age of cyber.

Attacks in the cyber domain are already occurring on a global scale with such frequency that several strategists have stated that the world is in a state of transition from the Cold War to the Code War. The frequency and likelihood of attacks in the cyber domain are increasing due to the lack of barriers for entry to the cyber battlefield, the gradually increasing ability to acquire cyber weapons, and the capacity to attack with relative anonymity. These factors present a growing threat to United States' national security and highlight the increased complexity of warfare caused by the cyber military revolution.

The cyber military revolution contains key attributes from each of the previous military revolutions. However, as the cyber case studies illustrate, the cyber revolution also has variations and additions to the attributes that increases its complexity and impact. An evaluation of the current United States framework of war will show that there is a conceptual gap between the current strategic framework and the means necessary to address the attributes of the cyber military revolution that have been identified.

CHAPTER 2: EVALUATING THE CURRENT FRAMEWORK OF WAR

The cyber military revolution was a direct result of the massive social and political changes enabled by the development and exponential integration of cyber technology into almost every aspect of society. Cyber technology and supporting infrastructures have completely restructured the methods and manners of domestic and international government, business, economics, politics, and social interaction. As with the previous military revolutions, changes of this scope should fundamentally alter the manner in which military organizations prepare for and conduct war.[1] Ultimately, the nation and the military that most quickly recognized a developing military revolution, understood the impacts on the framework of war, and adjusted their policies, strategy, and tactics was in the best position to increase their capacity to influence or coerce others to do their will. Conversely, failure to recognize the impacts and resulting changes to the framework of war that results from a military revolution (or even a lesser revolution in military affairs or attributes) increases a nation's vulnerability and sets the stage for defeat.

Despite recognition of the increasing importance and impact of the cyber domain, the United States has not fully recognized the fundamental shifts in the political, diplomatic, military, economic, informational, and social aspects of the current strategic environment that have occurred due to the cyber military revolution. The current United States framework of war is still firmly rooted in the theory espoused by Carl von Clausewitz in his classic *On War*. The inclusion and prominent placement of several of Clausewitz's dictums on the opening foundations page of Joint Publication 1 – *Doctrine*

---

[1] MacGregor Knox and Williamson Murray, *The Dynamics of Military Revolution, 1300-2050* (Cambridge: Cambridge University Press, 2001), 4.

for the Armed Forces of the United States, illustrates how strongly his theories continue to influence and shape the military's current framework of war:

> War is socially sanctioned violence to achieve a political purpose. In its essence, war is a violent clash of wills. War is a complex, human undertaking that does not respond to deterministic rules. Clausewitz described it as "the continuation of politics by other means." It is characterized by the shifting interplay of a trinity of forces (rational, nonrational, and irrational) connected by principal actors that comprise a social trinity of the people, military forces, and the government. He noted that the conduct of war combines obstacles such as friction, chance, and uncertainty. The cumulative effect of these obstacles is often described as "the fog of war." These observations remain true today and place a burden on the commander (CDR) to remain responsive, versatile, and adaptive in real time to seize opportunities and reduce vulnerabilities. This is the art of war.[2]

Clausewitz's Framework of War

Clausewitz developed his framework of war by using the dialectic method of reasoning. In the opening pages of *On War,* he establishes two theoretical bounds to help define the true reality of war. At one academic limit, Clausewitz presents his thesis that war at it most fundamental level is a duel between two opposing forces. At the opposing limit lies his antithesis that war is merely a continuation of policy by another means. Clausewitz synthesizes his evaluation into a framework of war that is based on the "fascinating trinity" theory that explains the unpredictable reality of war:

> War is thus more than a mere chameleon, because it changes its nature to some extent in each concrete case. It is also, however, when it is regarded as a whole and in relation to the tendencies that dominate within it, a fascinating trinity – composed of - primordial violence, hatred, and enmity, which are to be regarded as a blind natural force; the play of chance and probability, within which the creative spirit is free to roam; and its element of subordination, as an instrument of policy, which makes it subject to pure reason.

---

[2] U.S. Joint Chiefs of Staff, *Doctrine for the Armed Forces of the United States*, Joint Publication 1 (Washington DC: Joint Chiefs of Staff, 02 May 2007 Incorporating Change 1 20 March 2009) I-1.

The first of these three aspects concerns more the people, the second, more the commander and his army; the third, more the government.[3]

Realizing that the concept of the fascinating trinity may be difficult to comprehend, Clausewitz provided a model where each member of the trinity comprises a magnetic pole that exerts an attraction on a pendulum suspended above the trinitarian representation. Once set in motion, the position of the pendulum is an instantaneous summation of the war's current character based upon its relative position as determined by the current degree of attraction from each pole.

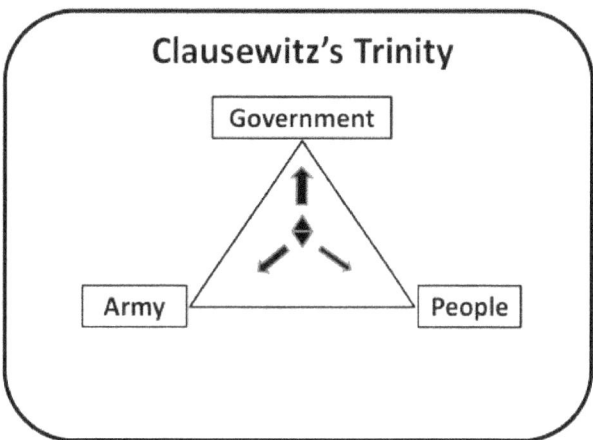

Figure 2.6 Clausewitz's Fascinating Trinity[4]

However, during war, the pendulum is an object in motion and the summation provided by its current position is only valid for a snapshot in time:

> As it enters a phase of its arc in which it is more strongly affected
> by one force than the others, it gains a momentum which carries it
> on into zones where the other forces can begin to exert their
> powers more strongly. The actual path of the suspended object is

[3] This paper uses Professor Christopher Bassford's translation of the Clausewitzian Trinity. See: Christopher Bassford, "Teaching the Clausewitzian Trinity,"Clausewitz.com. http://www.clausewitz.com/readings/Bassford/Trinity/TrinityTeachingNote.htm (accessed February 13, 2012).

[4] Figure developed by the author to help illustrate Clausewitz's trinity theory.

never determined by one force alone but by the interaction between them, which is forever and unavoidably shifting.[5]

Based upon that principle, Clausewitz felt his primary task was to develop a theory of war that strove to develop and maintain a balance between the three elements.[6] He also understood how difficult that task would be due to the "danger, chance, uncertainty, emotions, and differential talents of commanders" in war affecting the degree of pull and interaction between each of the elements of the trinity.[7]

Clausewitz uses only five paragraphs and approximately 300 words to present his foundational concept of the trinity.[8] Evaluation on the applicability of the concept of the trinity in the cyber age requires acknowledgement that there are numerous books, websites, and blogs by historians and military theorists that have polar opposite viewpoints. The crux of the debate is whether Clausewitz discovered a timeless model that adequately captured the interaction between a set number of elements in warfare, or if characteristics of past and likely future conflict expose the need to refine or replace the Clausewitz framework of war.

British military historian Sir Michael Howard, one of the primary authors for the most popular current translation of Clausewitz's *On War*, cautions that "to abstract war from the environment in which it is fought…is to ignore a dimension essential to the understanding, not simply of the wars themselves but of the societies which fought

[5] Christopher Bassford, "Clausewitz and His Works," Clausewitz.com, http://www.clausewitz.com/readings/Bassford/Cworks/Works.htm#Nature (accessed February 14, 2012).

[6] Carl von Clausewitz, *On War*, eds. and trans. Michael Howard and Peter Paret (Princeton: Princeton University Press, 1976), 76.

[7] Frans Osinga, *Science, Strategy and War: The Strategic Theory of John Boyd*. (Amsterdam: Eburon Academic Publishers, 2005), 21.

[8] Christopher Bassford, "Teaching the Clausewitzian Trinity," Clausewitz.com, http://www.clausewitz.com/readings/Bassford/Trinity/TrinityTeachingNote.htm (accessed February 13, 2012)

them."[9] Sir Michael Howard's admonition of the necessity of examining war in the context of the strategic environment in which it was fought also applies to evaluating attempts by theorists to extrapolate timeless frameworks, theories, and principles of warfare based on that timeframe. A well-developed framework and theory of warfare should explain and provide the foundation for a nation's armed forces to analyze and operate successfully in the current and expected future strategic environment. Thus, the key for evaluating the continued applicability of Clausewitz's framework of war is to determine whether the wholesale changes in the main aspects of the strategic environment have changed the definition and scope of the thesis, antithesis and eventual synthesis of his framework of war.[10]

Analyzing Clausewitz Thesis of War in the Age of Cyber

The definition of war is the underpinning of any framework of war. Clausewitz opens *On War* by immediately presenting his thesis that defines war at its most fundamental and unchanging level:

> War is nothing but a duel on a larger scale. Countless duels go to make up war, but picture of it as a whole can be formed by imaging a pair of wrestlers. Each tries through physical force to compel the other to do his will; his immediate aim is to throw his opponent in order to make him incapable of further resistance. War is thus an act of force to compel our enemy to do our will.[11]

As a lifelong professional soldier, Clausewitz understood that developing a definition and framework for war that would lead to battlefield success required more than just a

---

[9] Michael Howard, War in European History, (Oxford: University Press, 1979), as quoted in Anthony D. McIvor, *Rethinking the Principles of War,* (Annapolis: Naval Institute Press, 2005), x.

[10] Anthony D. McIvor, *Rethinking the Principles of War,* (Annapolis: Naval Institute Press, 2005), 169.

[11] Clausewitz, *On War,* 75.

devotion to the study of combat. It also required understanding of what causes wholesale

changes in the established order and the resulting changes in warfare over time.[12]

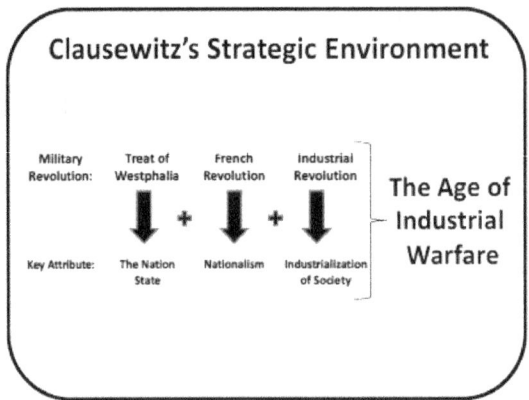

Figure 2.1 Clausewitz's Strategic Environment and the Age of Industrial

Warfare[13]

Clausewitz studied Napoleon's battles and the overall campaigns in depth to

formulate his understanding of how history shaped his strategic environment and

ultimately his thesis of war. He recognized that a state's ability to harness the zeal of

nationalism transforms the lethality of warfare. Additionally, he stated that advances

from the Industrial Revolution were able to field well-equipped armies primed for

battlefield success.[14] "Napoleon's successes, and also – ultimately – the measures

adopted by Napoleon's opponents in order to defeat the French," validated the

cumulative impact of the first three military revolutions on the character of war, and

---

[12] Anthony D. McIvor, *Rethinking the Principles of War* (Annapolis: Naval Institute Press, 2005), x.

[13] This figure was designed by the author to illustrate the military revolutions that had occurred before and during the lifetime of Clausewitz that affected the development of his theories of warfare.

[14] Alan D. Beyerchen, "Clausewitz, Nonlinearity, and the Importance of Imagery," Clausewitz.com, http://www.clausewitz.com/readings/Beyerchen/BeyerschenNonlinearity2.pdf, (accessed February 10, 2012).

ushered in the age of industrial warfare typified by nations dueling for victory through war.[15]

In describing war as fundamentally a duel between two warring parties, Clausewitz's context was two armies on a physical field of battle. As figure 2.2 illustrates, there are elements of the current cyber strategic environment that seem to fit the mold of Clausewitz's dialectic thesis of war. States are learning how to use the virtual domain to deliver "cyber fires" that support a duel between two states in a manner that Clausewitz would recognize.

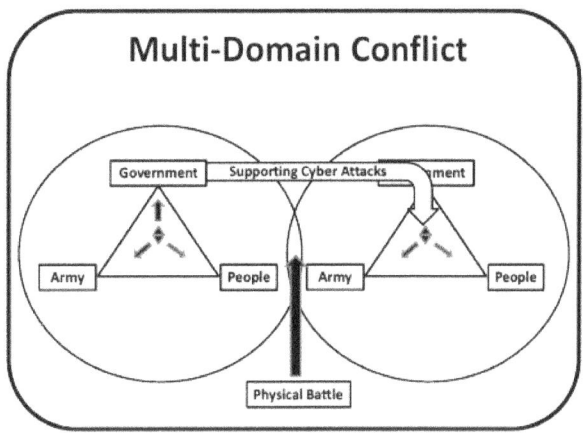

Figure 2.2 The Integration of Cyber into the Clausewitz's Dialectic of War[16]

In July of 2008, war erupted between Georgia and Russia over tensions caused by the breakaway territories of Ossetia and Abkhazia. The crisis escalated with Ossetian missile attacks on Georgian villages, which prompted Georgia to respond with bombing

---

[15] Alan D. Beyerchen, "Clausewitz, Nonlinearity, and the Importance of Imagery," Clausewitz.com. http://www.clausewitz.com/readings/Beyerchen/BeyerschenNonlinearity2.pdf. (accessed February 10, 2012).

[16] This figure was designed by the author to illustrate the how cyber operations could be used to support a form of warfare that Clausewitz would recognize through his 19th century lens.

raids on Ossetia's capital city and then a full-scale invasion on August 7th.[17] Russia seized this opportunity to insert itself into the conflict and used its army to rout and eject the Georgian army from South Ossetia rapidly.

The Russian attack actually started in the virtual domain. Prior to the Russian army's invading Ossetia, Russian hackers conducted denial-of-service attacks on Georgian government websites and defaced the website of the Georgian leader Mikheil Saakashvili.[18] While these cyber efforts seemed minor at first, they were actually probing attacks and preemptive strikes that identified vulnerabilities in the Georgian systems and laid the groundwork for increasingly sophisticated attacks.

The Russian hackers were able to overload the routers that provided Internet connectivity to Georgia and completely shut down Georgian ability to use their own domains to connect to outside news and information sources or even communicate via email. The Russian hackers were able to block every effort the Georgians made to reroute and restore Internet services by using botnets from computers in Canada, Turkey, and Estonia.[19]

Russian hackers were eventually able to trick the international banking system into thinking that it was under attack from Georgian banks. This resulted in the automatic removal of Georgian banking systems from the international system, effectively shutting down Georgia's ability to integrate with the global economy.[20] The net effect was that Russia was able to use the cyber domain to pull Georgian resources,

---

[17] Richard A. Clark and Robert K. Knake. *Cyber War: The Next Threat to National Security and What to do About it.* (New York: Haper Collins, 2010), 18.
[18] Ibid., 19.
[19] Ibid., 19.
[20] Ibid., 20.

efforts, and attention away from the armed invasion as they sought to re-establish their ability to communicate and integrate into the global commons.

Although this type of state-on-state conflict demonstrates that cyberwarfare can be a tool used by one or both parties dueling in combat, there are two elements at play within the cyber domain that provide a challenge to the dialectic thesis of Clausewitz's framework of war.

Clausewitz started his framework of war with the definition of war as essentially a duel on a much larger scale. As figure 2.3 illustrates, it would be more appropriate to equate the dialectical thesis of war in cyber age to the shootout at the OK Corral.

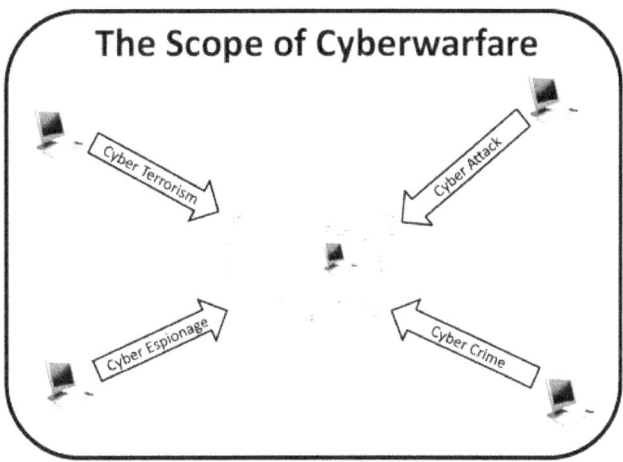

Figure 2.3 The Scope of Cyberwarfare[21]

In the cyber domain, similar techniques, programs, and methods will support and enable the simultaneous application of a full range of malicious activities against the United States from simple hacking to a terrorist attempt to takedown critical

---

[21] This figure was designed by the author to illustrate the need to expand the definition of war to include all actions taken in the cyber domain that have malicious intent against the United States. These actions must meet a threshold of damage or disruption that has not been adequately determined or defined yet in international law or joint doctrine.

infrastructure. Attempts to differentiate between these types of cyber activities and remove certain categories from the evaluation of the applicability of a framework of war because they do not fit traditional warfighting definitions can lead to defeat in a duel involving cyber.

For example, critics will dismiss cyber crime as being a law enforcement problem, and not a matter for the state or inclusion in a framework or theory of war. However, cyber crime is often the research and development arm of the cyber domain as it tests and refines malicious software for later use in more sophisticated cyber attacks that have a political or military objective.[22] Many of the hackers who participated in the Russian cyber attacks against Georgia are also involved in cyber crime.[23] The hackers just simply shifted the focus of their attacks, but not their methods. Federal Bureau of Investigations Director Robert Mueller recently highlighted the magnitude and growing likelihood of increased cooperation or mergers between cyber criminals and terrorists:

> Cyber crime is becoming a greater threat than terrorism. Be[coming] more dangerous to America than Al Qaeda…we expect, in a not so distant future, cyber threats will constitute the greatest danger to the country. Until now, the terrorists have not used the Internet to launch a large-scale cyber attack in the United States. But we cannot underestimate the intention of the terrorists.[24]

Despite the fact that over 120 nations are actively leveraging the Internet for political, military, and economic espionage activities, there is still a lack of international and domestic consensus or law on what constitutes an act of cyber war.[25] Debating about

---

[22] Jeffrey Carr, *Inside Cyber Warfare* (Sebastopol, CA: O'Reilly Media, 2010), 5.
[23] Ibid., 5.
[24] CWZ, "FBI expert calls for cyber warfare," CWZ.com, http://www.cyberwarzone.com/cyberwarfare/fbi-expert-calls-cyber-warfare?utm_source=twitterfeed&utm_medium=twitter, (accessed March 5, 2012).
[25] Carr, *Inside Cyber Warfare*, 1.

what to include under the umbrella of cyber warfare has led to a fractured defense that splits the oversight and defense responsibilities among multiple United States government agencies.

Based upon the campaigns in which he participated and studied, Clausewitz outlines the primary role in warfare for each member of the trinity throughout *On War*. For Clausewitz, each war is unique due to the non-linear relationship and interaction between the three elements of the trinity, but each member does have a principle function. In general, the state dictated the policy, the armed forces did the fighting, and the people supported the war effort by equipping the army with personnel and resources. Cyber warfare challenges the Clausewitizian paradigm in two primary ways. First, it has resulted in shifting or redefining roles and responsibilities between the members of the fascinating trinity as the United States attempts to duel in the cyber arena. When defending against cyber attacks, the United States Department of Defense has the responsibility to defend only the .mil domain, and the Department of Homeland Security has the responsibility to defend the rest of the federal government. The government and the military are attempting to protect their systems, but have left the policy and defense of the private sector to private corporations and even individuals. This exposes critical systems such the banking industry, transportation networks, and power infrastructures to attacks from foreign states, terrorists, and hackers. Richard Clark, former National Coordinator for Security, Infrastructure Protection, and Counterterrorism, provides an outstanding historical parallel that demonstrates the flaw in our current approach:

> At the beginning of the era of strategic nuclear war capability, the U.S. deployed thousands of air defense fighter aircraft and ground-based missiles to defend the population and the industrial base, not just to protect military facilities. Every major city was ringed with

Nike missile bases to shoot down Soviet bombers. At the beginning of the age of cyber war, the U.S. government is telling the population and industry to defend themselves. As one friend of mine asked, "Can you imagine if in 1958 the Pentagon told U.S. Steel and General Motors to go buy their own Nike missile to protect themselves?[26]

The second flaw further complicates the significant challenge that cyber warfare presents to Clausewitz's dialectic thesis of war. Clausewitz saw and based his definition of war through the lens of his time that was predominately a state-on-state conflict with a clearly indentified opponent. Figure 2.4 shows the results from a survey of over 500 security practitioners with an average of 9.57 years of experience. Over half of the surveyed organizations consisted of 5,000 or more employees. The chart provides a telling illustration on the current lack of ability to define one's opponent in the cyber duel.

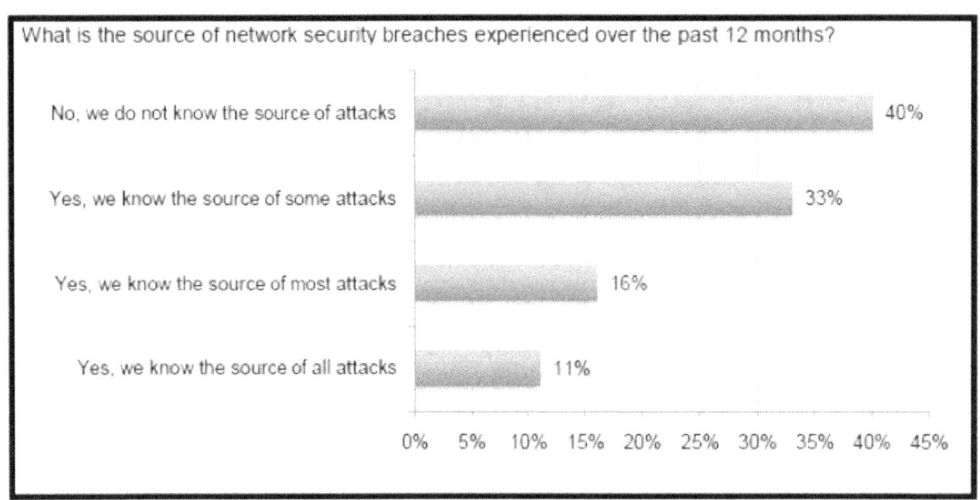

Figure 2.4 Identifying the Source of Cyber Attacks[27]

The inability to be able to identify and more importantly properly attribute acts of warfare to the correct adversary is an issue Clausewitz did not have to address in the

---

[26] Clark and Knake. *Cyber War*, 144.

[27] Mike Lennon, "Threat from Cyber Attack Nearing Statistical Certainty," Security Week.com. http://www.securityweek.com/threat-cyber-attacks-nearing-statistical-certainty, (Accessed February 16, 2012).

development of his theories. In his terms, one could be in a duel and you would know you were in a duel because of being shot at, but only 60 percent of the time could the identity of the shooter be apparent. This trend is getting worse. In recent congressional testimony regarding Chinese cyber capabilities, Richard Bejtlich, chief security officer of Mandiant, a computer-security company, highlighted that over 94 percent of the targeted companies were not aware that their computer systems were compromised until notified by outside security specialists. Worse, the average number of days between the start of the intrusion and detection was 416 days, well over a year.[28] This presents a challenge a new framework of war must address.

Analyzing Clausewitz's Antithesis of War in the Age of Cyber

Having defined his thesis on warfare, Clausewitz shifted to establishing the opposing antithesis based upon very early life experiences as well as the study of Napoleonic warfare. At the age of 12, while serving as a lance corporal in the Prussian army, Clausewitz gained his first exposure to the political aspects of warfare. His participation, observations, and study of the Prussian military campaigns of 1793 and 1794 led him to conclude that war was ultimately a political phenomenon. In 1792, the French declared war on Austria, which had recently signed a defensive alliance with Prussia. In this historical case, internal politics was the primary motivation for the French declaring war and it ultimately led to twenty-three years of war on the European continent. Prussia honored their defense alliance with Austria, but did not commit their full military resources to the war. Although the Prussians limited the size of their engagement, by 1795 they had won decisive victories over the French in Alsace and Saar

---

[28] Devlin Barrett, "U.S. Outgunned in Hacker War," WSJ.com, http://online.wsj.com/article/SB10001424052702304177104577307773326180032.html?mod=WSJ_hp_MIDDLENexttoWhatsNewsSecond, (accessed March 28, 2012)

and captured thousands of prisoners.[29] Despite their battlefield successes, Clausewitz recognized that Prussia had paid a high price in casualties and the extensive draw on the national treasury, but in the end had achieved no political return.[30]

Clausewitz based the antithesis of his framework of war on his view that there can be no separation of any aspect of warfare from the overarching political purpose: "We see, therefore, that war is not merely an act of policy but a true political instrument, a continuation of political intercourse, carried on with other means."[31] For Clausewitz, the political objective as decided by the state will determine the supporting military objective and the amount of effort a nation will exert to achieve both objectives.[32]

The conventional understanding of Clausewitz's dictum that war is "the continuation of policy" by other means holds that politics/policies drive war in a linear fashion.[33] As depicted in Figure 2.5, the state would determine how far down the road to war they are willing to travel, and would decide if war would be the policy they deem necessary to address and solve the crisis.

---

[29] Clausewitz, *On War*, 5-7.
[30] Ibid., 75.
[31] Ibid., 87.
[32] Ibid., 81.
[33] Alan D. Beyerchen, "Clausewitz, Nonlinearity, and the Importance of Imagery," Clausewitz.com, http://www.clausewitz.com/readings/Beyerchen/BeyerschenNonlinearity2.pdf, (accessed February 10, 2012)

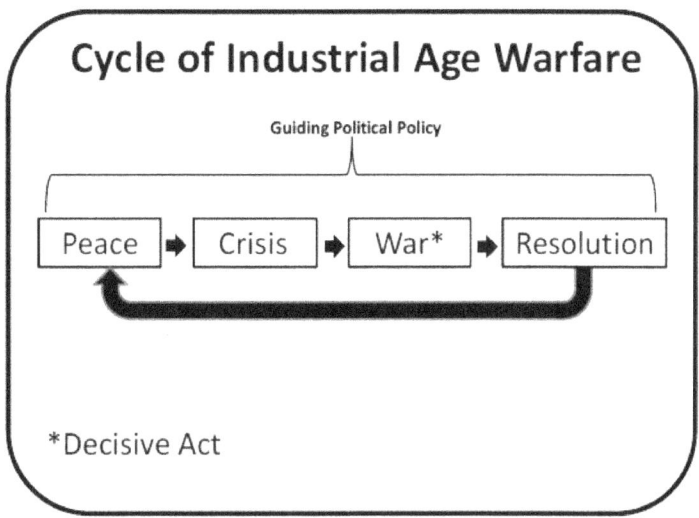

Figure 2.5 Cycle of Industrial Age Warfare[34]

Clausewitz reinforced that war, once chosen as the state's policy, would be the decisive act to resolve the crisis. However, he repeatedly cautions that attention on the conduct of the war and achieving the military objectives cannot remove or overshadow the guiding political focus: "war should never be thought of as something autonomous but always as an instrument of policy."[35]

In contrast to the focus on state-on-state conflict that forms the basis of Clausewitz's framework of war, the cyber military revolution has created a strategic environment where war has a much higher resemblance to the characteristics and facets of the pre-Westphalian state-on-state era, than the battlefields of 18th – 20th century.

> For a thousand years after the fall of Rome armed conflict was waged by different kinds of social entities. Among them were barbarian tribes, the Church, feudal barons of every rank, free cities, even private individuals. Nor were the "armies" of the

---

[34] This figure was developed by the author to illustrate the linear nature of industrial warfare.
[35] Clausewitz, *On War*, 81.

period anything like those we know today; indeed, it is difficult to find a word that would do them justice.[36]

Figure 2.6 illustrates how the low cost, low risk, and low barrier to entry into the cyber domain has resulted in an increasing complex strategic environment with social entities as diverse as the those identified above.

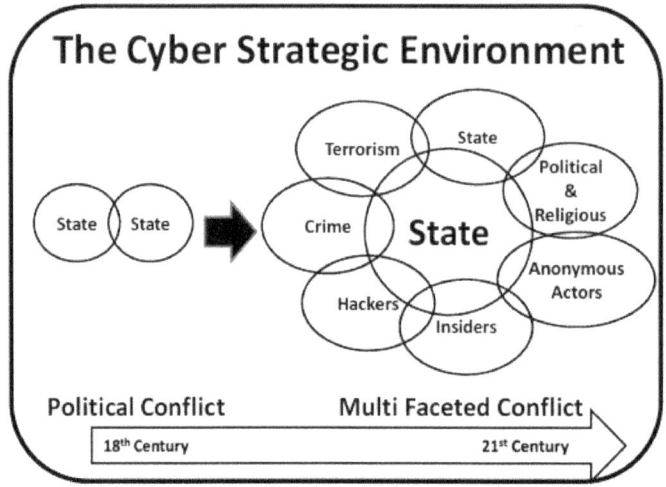

Figure 2.6 The Cyber Strategic Environment[37]

The ability of this variety of actors to conduct continuous worldwide operations at the speed of light within the cyber domain has shattered the notion of a linear road to war and confrontation between two specified forces. Although there will be instances of cyber attacks being used to support a more traditional form of war, in today's multi-faceted strategic environment cyber attacks are diverse, unrelenting, and are often difficult to identify the true adversary and their intent.

---

[36] Martin Van Creveld, *The Transformation of War*. (New York: Free Press, 1991), 52.

[37] This figure was developed by the author to depict the increasing challenge of operating in the contemporary strategic environment due to the exponentially increasing number of actors that may have convergent, divergent, or unknown objectives.

The Cyber Military Revolution meets the Fascinating Trinity

These shifts are redefining the interplay of the forces internal to Clausewitz's trinity. As the Arab Spring demonstrated, the cyber domain and social media are strengthening the pull of the irrational element of the trinity. Radical redirection of both national and international policy can come from a single individual posting a video on YouTube.com that goes viral and inflames the passion of a nation or appeals to broader pan nationalism. Militaries are becoming vulnerable to degrading or debilitating cyber attacks as they increase their dependence on the cyber domain to conduct wartime operations. Many states are recognizing that the cyber domain is radically reshaping information distribution and is breaking down the final barriers of information control for repressive regimes. For example, the Iranian government is reportedly working on a "clean Internet" that will block and replace content from sources deemed objectionable by the state." Part of this effort would be to replace search engines like Google or Bing with state-sanctioned services. Service would also require individual registration for access, making it much easier for the state to monitor Internet activity.[38]

Some theorists argue that these factors are only increasing the role of friction, chance, and unpredictability with the non-linear interaction of the trinity. Others will argue that the era of industrial warfare is over, and that a new generation of warfare based on terrorism, insurgencies and/or cyber has completely replaced the Clausewitzian paradigm of state-on-state conflict. The traditional characteristics that make up the current paradigm of warfare are decreasing and may eventually disappear. Warfare is

---

[38] Andrew Tarantola, "Iran Denies It's Shutting Down the Internet in August, Merely Building a New One Next March," Gizmodo.com, http://gizmodo.com/5900876/iran-denies-its-shutting-down-the-Internet-in-august-merely-building-a-new-one-next-march, (accessed April 14, 2012)

shifting from indentified front lines, campaigns, and clearly identified combatants to violent and non-violent engagement that is not limited by territorial boundaries and economic sovereignty of nations. [39]

Figure 2.7 illustrates that what has happened is actually a synthesis of the two opposing viewpoints.

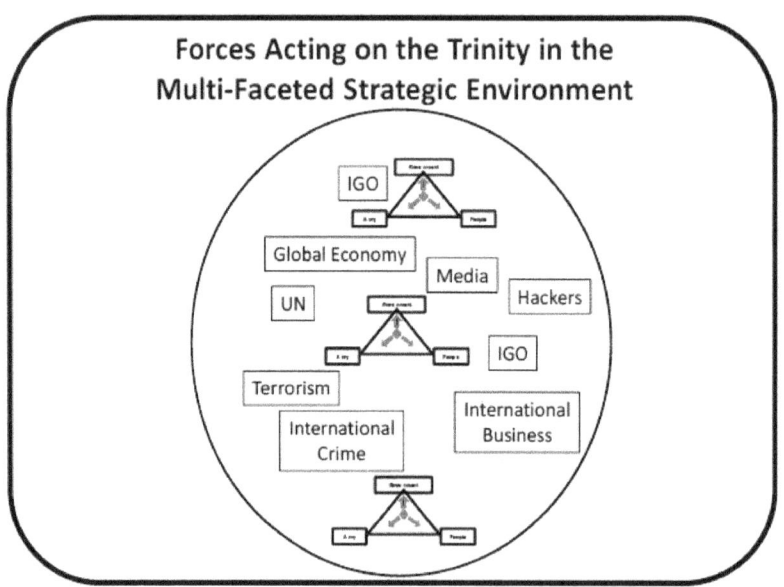

Figure 2.7 Forces Acting on the Trinity in the Multi-Faceted Strategic Environment[40]

Some states will continue to engage in a trinitarian manner Clausewitz would recognize. However, by reducing or even eliminating the relevance of physical

[39] Frans Osinga, *Science, Strategy and War: The Strategic Theory of John Boyd.* (Amsterdam: Eburon Academic Publishers, 2005), 29.

[40] This figure was developed by the author to demonstrate the various forces that are impacting the character of warfare simultaneously in today's and tomorrow's strategic environment. Several states may interact in a trinitarian manner Clausewitz would recognize, yet cyber has removed physical proximity as a factor in engagement between traditional nation states. In addition to the standard pull that each element of the Clausewitz's trinity has on warfare, the additional groups, organizations, or individuals identified in this figure are all exerting a force on the character of conflict within today's strategic environment.

proximity, cyber warfare has provided states the ability to conduct instantaneous global strikes against any nation wired to the Internet. Additionally, unlike warfare in Clausewitz's era, the cyber domain allows states to attack with relative anonymity and little fear of retribution, which complicates an opposing states ability to deter or defeat cyber attacks.[41]

Non-trinitarian forces such as anonymous super-empowered individuals, terrorists, transnational criminal organizations, religious groups, insiders, and hackers are all working to exploit existing vulnerabilities in the cyber domain to pursue malevolent objectives with widely diverse purposes against the United States (and others). These non-state actors are able to utilize several aspects of the cyber battlefield that are distinctive from what Clausewitz observed and studied to develop his framework of war.

Historian Michael Handel postulates that not anticipating these diverse actors and their impacts on the conduct of war is a likely result of Clausewitz's general neglect of the economic and material dimension of war. Handel felt Clausewitz' main objective with *On War* was to write a book for military leaders that focused on how to fight and win, with the assumption that the state has already addressed the necessary material and economic preparations and continuing requirements. Failing to include what Handel describes as a necessary fourth dimension to the Trinity of Warfare, lessens the understanding and incorporation of the impact that material, economics, and technology have on warfare.[42] All three of those factors are the key characteristics of the cyber military revolution.

---

[41] Kenneth Geers, "Sun Tzu and Cyber War," Cooperative Cyber Defence Centre of Excellence, http://www.ccdcoe.org/articles/2011/Geers_SunTzuandCyberWar.pdf, (Accessed February 16, 2012).

[42] Michael I. Handel, *Masters of War*, (London: Routledge, 2005), 108-109.

Cyber combat is also shifting the moral components of war. Clausewitz developed his framework based upon the brutality of war: "If one side uses force without compunction, undeterred by the bloodshed it involves, while the other side refrains, the first will gain the upper hand."[43] He further theorized that advances in technology will only further increase bloodshed necessary to achieve the objective of war, and thus weigh on the calculus of a state's decision to seek war as the policy to further their objectives:

> The invention of gunpowder and the constant improvement in firearms are enough in themselves to show that the advance of civilization has done nothing practical to alter or deflect the impulse to destroy the enemy, which is the very idea of war.[44]

In contrast, advances in civilization through the development and capabilities of cyber technologies are removing moral inhibitions to war conducted through the virtual domain. The real or perceived lack of human suffering for most forms of cyber attack, has increased the likelihood of occurrence due to the reduced risk of provoking international outrage, backlash, or possibly even reprisal attacks.[45]

As figure 2.6 and the case studies in Chapter 1 illustrate, cyber attacks are persistent, varied, and have changed the character of war sufficiently to challenge the applicability of Clausewitz's framework of war to current and future conflict. External non-state and non-trinitarian factors are increasingly dominating or controlling the path of a pendulum swinging through the elements of the trinity to the degree that Clausewitz's model needs replacement as a foundational element for joint doctrine.

---

[43] Clausewitz, *On War*, 75-76.
[44] Ibid., 76.
[45] Kenneth Geers, "Sun Tzu and Cyber War," Cooperative Cyber Defence Centre of Excellence, http://www.ccdcoe.org/articles/2011/Geers_SunTzuandCyberWar.pdf, (Accessed February 16, 2012).

CHAPTER 3: THE CORE ELEMENT FOR A NEW FRAMEWORK OF WAR

The case studies highlighting recent acts of cyber warfare demonstrate the fundamental changes that have occurred and are continuing to occur in the character and conduct of war because of the cyber military revolution. These studies have also identified conceptual gaps between a framework of war based upon the theories of Clausewitz and a structure that is sufficient to guide the development of strategy, doctrine and operations in the cyber age. A new methodology of war must address these challenges and have at its heart a fundamental core element that provides warfighters a theory that will increase the nation's opportunity to prevail in warfare "in the age of cyber." This chapter introduces Colonel John Boyd's OODA loop as the core element required in an updated framework of war that will address the changing character of warfare and the conceptual gaps that exist in the current structure.

Colonel John Boyd and the Observe-Orient-Decide-Act Loop

United States Air Force Colonel John Boyd was a legendary fighter pilot and self-taught military theorist who developed a philosophy of warfare that, at its core, is sufficiently flexible and adaptable to integrate changes in the shifting character of war:

> …in order to win, we should operate at a faster tempo or rhythm than our adversaries – or better yet, get inside the adversary's observation – orientation – decision – action time (OODA) cycle or loop. Getting inside your adversaries decision cycle makes you appear ambiguous and generates confusion and disorder. This leads to the adversary's inability to understand his environment and develop a proper mental image to develop options to compete against the patterns they are trying to defeat.[1]

---

[1] John Boyd, "Patterns of Conflict," DNI net, http://www.dnipogo.org/boyd/patterns_ppt.pdf (accessed February 21, 2012).

Some scholars and military theorists have attacked the applicability of Boyd's OODA loop to serve as the core element for a framework of war above the tactical or operational level. British Officer Jim Storr wrote an award-winning essay denying OODA loops exist at the strategic level. His argument was the extended time frame required for decisions and actions at the strategic level prevented formulating rapid decision cycles.[2]

Failure to recognize the effectiveness of Boyd's OODA loop as a core element of a war framework that supports strategy, doctrine, and operations from the strategic to tactical level often comes from a general misunderstanding and an oversimplification of the OODA loop as illustrated in figured 3.1.

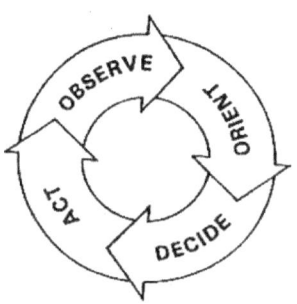

Figure 3.1 Oversimplification of Boyd's OODA Loop[3]

The OODA loop is not a one- dimensional simple four-step cycle of decision making: observing an adversary's actions, becoming oriented to the possible enemy courses of action, making a decision, taking action and then repeating the cycle as the

[2] Frans Osinga, *Science, Strategy and War: The Strategic Theory of John Boyd.* (Amsterdam: Eburon Academic Publishers, 2005), 21.

[3] TDAXP, Ph.D, "Variations of the OODA Loops 2, The Naive Boydian Loop," TDAXP.com, http://www.tdaxp.com/archive/2006/05/31 (accessed February 21, 2012).

environment changes from the effects of the action taken.[4] Too often, military decision makers and strategists discussing the OODA loop tout this misconception and expound on the fact that the most important facet in application of the OODA loop is to complete the full cycle in a linear fashion as fast as possible.[5]

The OODA loop is much more than a decision cycle model; it is a synthesis of Boyd's philosophy of war and patterns in conflict that he identified as essential to prevail at all levels of war. Historian Colin Gray would agree, and ranks Boyd amongst the greatest theorists of the 20th century:

> John Boyd deserves at least honorable mention of his discovery of the 'OODA Loop'...allegedly comprising a universal logic....Boyd's loop can apply to the operational, strategic, and political levels of war...The OODA loop may appear too humble to merit categorization as grand theory, but that is what it is. It has an elegant simplicity, an extensive domain of applicability, and contains a high quality of insight about strategic essentials...[6]

Figure 3.2 is a more accurate and complete depiction of Boyd's OODA loop. The competitive power of the OODA loop comes from the simultaneous observation of the environment looking for mismatches between conception of the world and reality, then orienting or re-orienting to the ambiguous, confusing, or changing situation, developing the best course of action to pursue, and then acting upon it. It is not just the speed of getting through the entire cycle that gives the OODA loop its power and agility; it is the time it takes to transition "from one orientation state to another."[7]

---

[4] Robert Coram. *Boyd: The Fighter Pilot Who Changed the Art of War*, (Boston: Little, Brown, 2002), 328.

[5] Ibid., 335.

[6] Osinga, *Science, Strategy and War: The Strategic Theory of John Boyd*, 3.

[7] Chet Richards, *Certain to Win: The Strategy of John Boyd, Applied to Business*, ([Philadelphia: Xlibris, 2004), 63.

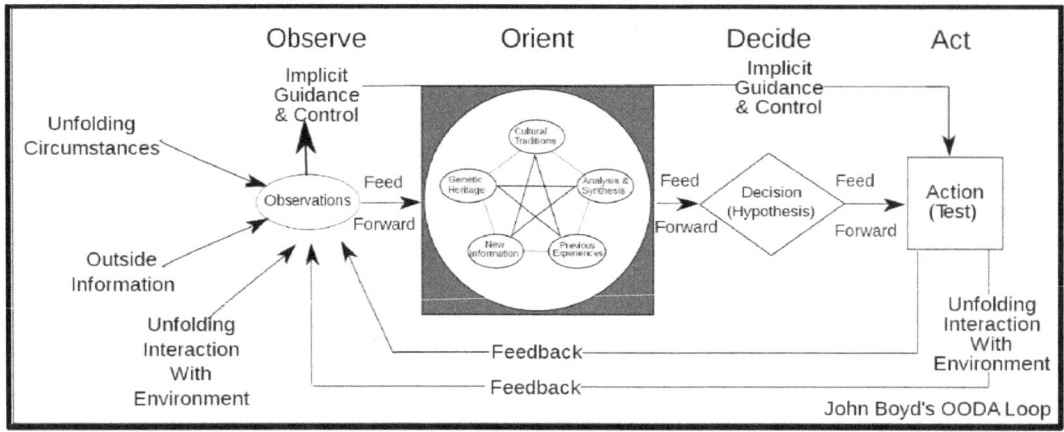

Figure 3.2 Boyd's Observe-Orient-Decide-Act (OODA) Loop[8]

To understand and apply the OODA loop as the core element of a new framework of war requires a brief exploration of the concepts and principles Boyd used to develop his philosophy of war and how those factors influenced the development and proper application of the OODA loop in the cyber age.

The Power of Observation

The development of Boyd's philosophy of war began early in his military career as a fighter pilot in the Korean War. During that war, the United States F-86 averaged a 10:1 kill ratio over the Soviet built MiG-15 despite the MiG's being faster, having a higher operational ceiling, and turning more tightly than the F-86.[9] The post-war analysis, the quality of which is still touted in some academic circles today, highlighted ability to achieve such a domineering kill ratio (792 MiGs shot down compared to 78 F-86 losses) solely as a result of the superior skill and training of American pilots.[10] Boyd refused to accept that analysis. He spent a decade studying detailed analysis of each

[8] Osinga, *Science, Strategy and War: The Strategic Theory of John Boyd*, 270.
[9] Grant Hammond, *The Mind of War, John Boyd and American Security*, (Washington, D.C.: Smithsonian Institution, 2004), 35.
[10] Coram, *Boyd: The Fighter Pilot Who Changed the Art of War*, 55.

Korean War air-to-air engagement to find solid rationale that would explain how often outnumbered and outperformed F-86s were able to achieve such dominating kill ratios over the MiG-15s.

The conventional judgment of the day was that an aircraft's worth was based upon how high, how far, and how fast it could go, but Boyd's analysis demonstrated his need to broaden the search for defining variables that were beyond the traditional ways used to measure the strength of an opponent.[11] He was able to determine that although United States pilot training was superior to North Korean pilots; two other factors were the primary reasons behind such dramatic combat results.

First, the F-86 had a bubble canopy that offered the United States pilots superior visibility and the ability to observe the entire air-to-air engagement. The MiG-15 pilots only had a limited forward view and thus their view of the engagement and their resulting decisions were restricted based upon what they could see in their forward aspect. This gave United States pilots the ability to build a higher level of situational awareness, orienting them to the larger battle and enabling better decision-making based upon having an expanded knowledge of the total air-to-air environment.[12] Second, the F-86 had hydraulically assisted flight controls while the MiG-15 did not. As Boyd discovered, this gave the F-86 the ability to transition from one maneuver to the next faster than the MiG-15. The combination of better training, outstanding visibility, and powered flight controls often put the MiG-15 pilot in a position where he was completely reactive to the decisions of the F-86 pilot.

---

[11] Hammond, *The Mind of War, John Boyd and American Security*, 35.
[12] Ibid., 35.

Boyd's discoveries led him to establish observation as a key foundation for his philosophy of war and it would eventually become the first element in his OODA loop. In air-to-air combat, the situation is fluid and chaotic. Pilots build their situational awareness and develop a mental picture of the airspace and action not only based upon what they see, but also upon what they are hearing on the radio from ground or air controllers. Additionally, the various systems in the aircraft help detect and display what is occurring. Removal or degradation of any of these elements will reduce the ability of a pilot to construct an accurate mental picture and properly orient during the air-to-air battle.

To support a framework of war for the cyber age, the observation phase is a continual scan of the strategic environment in order to identify the possible factors and variables influencing or affecting the United States from a growing, interconnected, and complex global system in both the physical and virtual domains. In addition to identifying traditional nation-state allies and potential opponents, the objective of strategic observation is to determine whether anonymous actors, super-empowered individuals, terrorists, transnational criminal organizations, religious groups, insiders, hackers, pan-nationalists or social media-driven movements are active. It then needs to determine how the active actors are affecting the strategic environment and attempt to determine whether their actions are clouding or distorting the observation.

During observation, it is critical to maintain awareness for adversaries that are increasingly seeking to undermine, degrade, disrupt, and in the future, potentially defeat the United States through cyber strategic paralysis rather than physical destruction.[13] The cyber domain is becoming the great equalizer in future warfare. The conventional

[13] Osinga, *Science, Strategy and War: The Strategic Theory of John Boyd*, 53.

domination of the United States, as demonstrated in Operation Desert Storm, Operation Enduring Freedom, and Operation Iraqi Freedom, has significantly reduced the probability of large-scale and state-on-state conventional warfare. Current and potential future adversaries will be extremely reluctant to attempt a "head-to-head" physical engagement with United States conventional forces because they know it will result in an overwhelming defeat.[14]

The nation's current and potential future adversaries are searching for different methods to achieve their desired objectives. Terrorism is one avenue of approach that adversaries use to bypass the United States' conventional dominance. The cyber domain offers a potentially more destructive avenue of approach to attack American mental and moral dimensions. Doing so would threaten United States intellectual thinking power and creativity and could disintegrate a national willingness to resist. These are new and novel threats that do not conform to the traditional worldview of defining or searching for threats based solely upon the ability to conduct physical damage. Successful observation in today's strategic environment must include equal scans of the physical, mental, and moral dimensions.

The Power of Maneuverability

The next event in Boyd's Air Force career that would significantly shape his philosophy of war came from a breakthrough he had while pursuing an engineering master's degree program at Georgia Tech. While studying the laws of thermodynamics, Boyd realized that power and airspeed were not what enabled a pilot to outmaneuver

---

[14] Mc Ivor, Anthony. *Rethinking the Principles of War*. (MD: Naval Institute Press, 2005}, 115.

another aircraft; rather the thermodynamic laws regarding conservation and energy had a much greater factor on determining success.[15]

Boyd expanded on this concept and developed it into the energy maneuverability (EM) theory. EM provided a mathematical method of plotting the maneuverability of an aircraft at different altitudes, g forces, and turning rates that allowed the direct comparison of two dissimilar aircraft engaged in air-to-air combat. These comparisons enabled Boyd to determine where one type of aircraft could gain advantage over another and what changes in aircraft design would increase the maneuverability and lethality of United States fighter aircraft.[16] Boyd ultimately received the Harold Brown Award, the highest scientific award given by the United States Air Force, for the EM theory. In presenting the award, the Secretary of the Air Force noted the citation that gave Boyd credit for developing a theory that gave the United States fighter aircraft force a combat advantage for decades to come.[17]

Boyd expanded the concepts of his EM theory to warfare in general and developed a greater appreciation for the ability to outmaneuver and mentally defeat an opponent in warfare. The ability to outmaneuver adversaries mentally became the basis for the development of the second element of the OODA loop – orient – and ultimately the strategic aim of his philosophy of war.[18]

Orientation: The Ultimate Power of the OODA Loop

---

[15] Hammond, *The Mind of War, John Boyd and American Security*, 54.
[16] Ibid., 57.
[17] Coram. *Boyd: The Fighter Pilot Who Changed the Art of War*, 310.
[18] John Boyd, "Patterns of Conflict," DNI.net, http://www.dnipogo.org/boyd/patterns_ppt.pdf (accessed February 21, 2012).

The orientation phase is what gives Boyd's concept its power. The objective of the orientation phase is to interpret and decide what the observed information means and convert that information into a body of knowledge.[19] The objective of the process was to have a more relevant interpretation of the actual environment, based upon a better ability to discover and synthesize linkages and relationships between the variables and factors observed, one's genetic heritage, social environment, and prior experiences.[20] This enables the formulation of the best options or alternatives upon which to base a decision and take the necessary actions to implement the decision.

It is important to highlight that taking an action does not necessarily complete an OODA loop cycle. As figure 3.2 illustrates, the OODA loop is a non-linear process where orientation shapes observation, shapes decision, shapes action and in turn is shaped by the feedback and other phenomena coming into the observation window.[21]

The proper application of the OODA loop in a non-linear fashion is a key to success in the complex and challenging cyber environment. It provides commanders the necessary agility to keep their orientation well matched to the real world, which will be increasingly imperative as innovation in the cyber domain continues to inject ambiguity, confusion, and rapid change into the strategic environment that could lead to disorientation.[22]

Cyber space is a man-made domain, unique from the physical restrictions that limit innovation in the land, sea, air and space warfighting domains. Computing power

---

[19] N. Nayab, "Exploring the OODA Loop with Examples," Bright Hub, http://www.brighthub.com/office/project-management/articles/105998.aspx (accessed February 24, 2012)

[20] Richards, *Certain to Win: The Strategy of John Boyd, Applied to Business*, 62.

[21] John Boyd, "Patterns of Conflict," DNI net, http://www.dnipogo.org/boyd/patterns_ppt.pdf (accessed February 21, 2012).

[22] Richards, *Certain to Win: The Strategy of John Boyd, Applied to Business*, 62.

has a proven history of doubling in capacity every two years. As a result, cyber technological development is far outpacing man's ability to innovate, and therefore is not a physical limitation or restriction on the rate of change possible.[23] American scientist, author, and futurist Ray Kurzweil, predicts that this exponential growth trend will continue. He theorizes that as computing power continues to improve at an exponential rate, within a few decades machine intelligence will exceed human intelligence.[24] This explosive rate of change and associated development introduces a proliferation of technologies that will require continuous orientation and re-orientation to the strategic environment.

As the case studies in Chapter One described, cyber technology has already provided a method of maneuver that can shatter the cohesion of critical national systems such as banking, transportation, communication and stock exchanges. For now, these actions may be temporarily disruptive, but if these meteoric development rates continue, in the future they could lead to opportunities for a decisive attack that could cause significant national paralysis.

Recognizing and developing the best decisions and actions to prevent these types of decisive attacks necessitates incorporating the OODA loop into an updated framework of war. This will reinforce the need to re-orient constantly to the changing character of war due to the phenomenal rate of cyber innovation. The objective of the commander must be to keep one's orientation intact, while taking active measures to disrupt or destroy the orientation of the multi-faceted adversaries acting against the United States.

---

[23] Franklin D. Kramer, Stuart H. Starr, and Larry K. Wentz, *Cyberpower and National Security* (Washington D.C.: National Defense University Press, 2009), 5.
[24] Ray Kurzweil, "The Law of Accelerating Returns," Kurzweil Accelerating Intelligence, http://www.kurzweilai.net/the-law-of-accelerating-returns (accessed February 3, 2012).

This will allow commanders and warfighters to outmaneuver an adversary mentally, morally, and physically by generating confusion, disorder, and destruction as required in order to deter or defeat his efforts to do the nation harm.

CHAPTER 4: RECOMMENDATION AND CONCLUSION

As the case studies and analysis in Chapter 1 illustrate, the creation of the cyber domain has ushered in sufficiently profound changes in society and warfare to merit classification as a military revolution. A new interconnected civilization is arising from a society in the midst of a radical transformation, all resulting from the continued integration of cyber technology into domestic and international governance, business, economics, politics, and social interaction. As with the previous five military revolutions, the changes in warfare marshaled in by the cyber age should have forced the United States to evaluate whether current joint doctrine provides a framework of war that is sufficiently robust to guide strategy, doctrine development, and military operations at all levels. Unfortunately, that has not occurred.

Despite current and past Presidents and Secretaries of Defense repeatedly advocating the need to prevail in the cyber domain in documents as significant as the recent 2012 National Strategic Guidance, there has not been necessary revision to the current framework of war as articulated in the United States military's capstone Joint Publication (reposted for ease of reference):

> War is socially sanctioned violence to achieve a political purpose.
> In its essence, war is a violent clash of wills. War is a complex,
> human undertaking that does not respond to deterministic rules.
> Clausewitz described it as "the continuation of politics by other
> means." It is characterized by the shifting interplay of a trinity of
> forces (rational, non-rational, and irrational) connected by
> principal actors that comprise a social trinity of the people, military
> forces, and the government. He noted that the conduct of war
> combines obstacles such as friction, chance, and uncertainty. The
> cumulative effect of these obstacles is often described as "the fog
> of war." These observations remain true today and place a burden
> on the commander (CDR) to remain responsive, versatile, and

adaptive in real time to seize opportunities and reduce vulnerabilities. This is the art of war.[1]

A revised framework of war should incorporate the key attributes of the cyber military revolution and integrate Boyd's OODA loop as the core foundational element to address the shortcomings identified with the continued use of Clausewitz's theory of warfare as the framework's foundation. The following is the recommended revision to the United States framework of war to be included in the next rewrite of Joint Publication-1 (Italicized indicates new or edited content from current version):

> *War is no longer primarily a periodic violent clash of wills between opponents relying upon force in the physical domain. War is shifting to continual non-violent confrontations among numerous opponents in the virtual cyber domain that will have intermittent episodes of related or non-related violent conflicts in the physical domain. The participants in war have expanded from established nation-states or powerful non-state groups, such as transnational terrorists attempting to impose a known will, to a diverse set of actors that may have divergent, convergent, or unknown objectives.* War is a complex, human undertaking that does not respond to deterministic rules. *War is no longer a process of continual mutual adaptation, of give and take, move and countermove in a relatively consistent strategic environment with each side seeking a massive decisive event. War is the unrelenting collision of actors' observation-orientation-decision-action (OODA) decision loops where each side is seeking to penetrate the moral-mental-physical being of their opponents to dissolve their moral fiber, disorient their mental images, disrupt their operations, and overload their systems. War is now a process of agility—placing a burden on the commanders to maximize their situational awareness, continuously update one's worldview to overcome the ambiguity, confusion, and rapid change in the dynamically complex strategic environment.* This is the art of war.[2]

[1] U.S. Joint Chiefs of Staff, *Doctrine for the Armed Forces of the United States,* Joint Publication 1 (Washington DC: Joint Chiefs of Staff, 02 May 2007 Incorporating Change 1 20 March 2009) I-1.

[2] This recommended framework is a synthesis of the author's analysis of the cyber case studies in Chapter One, and the underlining concepts of Colonel John Boyds philosophy war. John Boyd, "Patterns of Conflict," DNI net, http://www.dnipogo.org/boyd/patterns_ppt.pdf (accessed February 21, 2012).

The recommended revised framework of war starts out with the immediate emphasis on one key attribute of the cyber military revolution - the splintering effect on warfare caused by the introduction of the virtual domain. As current combat operations in Afghanistan, Libya, and possibly Syria, demonstrate, there will still be conflict in the physical domain. However, the ease of entry, low risk of detection or immediate identification, and increasing potential of significant economic and infrastructure damage is shifting the primary method of warfare from the physical to the virtual domain. Several of the case studies analyzed in Chapter 1 show that several nations, groups, and hackers have already successfully demonstrated the ability to bypass conventional strength to attack, destabilize, degrade, or shut down vital portions of an adversary's critical economic infrastructure directly, including vital banking systems and stock exchanges using relatively simple botnet attacks. Unfortunately, attacks such as the Stuxnet virus are demonstrating that we have seen only the tip of the iceberg regarding the ability to use the cyber domain as the sole method for causing physical destruction to critical infrastructure. Finally, the integration of the cyber domain with attacking physical forces, as in the Israeli raid on the suspected Syrian reactor, demonstrates a possible course of warfare triggered by the introduction of the cyber domain and the next evolution of combined arms warfare, the key attribute from the third military revolution.

The second item of immediate emphasis in the opening of the proposed framework is the recognition that warfare is shifting from the current linear paradigm of peace-crisis-war-peace, to a continuous confrontation in the virtual domain with occasional accompanying episodes of violent conflict in the physical domain. This shift is primarily the result of the explosive expansion of the multi-faceted actors ranging from the individual hacker to a first-world nation-state where both might have equal ability to shape, influence, and attack in the cyber domain. As illustrated in Chapter 2, the diverse set of actors continuously engaged against the United States in the cyber domain with malicious divergent, convergent, or unknown objectives has created an interplay of forces that includes, but goes far beyond, the elements of Clausewitz's trinity of forces.

This interplay of increasingly diverse and growing non-trinitarian actors is the primary reason for not including whole or elements of the first sentence from the old framework within the proposed revision. "War is socially sanctioned violence to achieve a political purpose,"[3] implies a linear framework of war where a government is required to seek legitimacy or have a rationale for pursing its political purpose through violent action. Nations are struggling to determine how much social sanction is required to pursue offensive action in the cyber domain. Compounding that challenge is the growing number of non-trinitarian actors that are not limited by the need for social sanctions to support their malicious objectives and operations within the cyber domain. As a result, the new framework of war recognizes that violent and non-violent clashes of will do occur, but does not impose a socially sanctioned caveat to a characterization of war that fails to apply to the majority of actors that acting within the strategic environment.

The proposed new framework of war does retain the sentence that reinforces the concept that war is a complex human undertaking that does not respond to deterministic rules. Both Clausewitz and Boyd would agree and did advocate this principle. In the cyber military revolution era, it is imperative not to get fixated on the promises of

---

[3] U.S. Joint Chiefs of Staff, *Doctrine for the Armed Forces of the United States*, Joint Publication 1 (Washington DC: Joint Chiefs of Staff, 02 May 2007 Incorporating Change 1 20 March 2009) I-1.

technology and to heed the admonition of Colonel John Boyd that, "Machines don't fight wars, people do."[4]

The shift of warfare towards continuous engagement in the virtual domain is often accompanied by operations in the physical domain. Coupled with the multi-faceted actors with diverse and possibly unknown objectives, this shift results in a constantly changing, ambiguous, chaotic, and complex strategic environment. As the Chapter 3 analysis of the development of Boyd's philosophy of war determined, the incorporation of the Boyd's OODA loop will provide the necessary core element for an effective new framework of war. The OODA loop provides the philosophy and methodology to maximize the development of one's situational awareness in order to construct the most accurate mental model of the strategic environment as possible, assisting in the development of a decision and taking an action. More importantly, multiple loops may occur within the OODA loop simultaneously with the objective of orienting and re-orienting to the dynamically complex environment as fast as possible.

The key aspect of the proposed framework is recognition that war is the "unrelenting collision" of the OODA loops from all of the multi-faceted actors from both the cyber and physical domain. The collision of OODA loops emanating from the diverse actors operating within the strategic environment will produce what Clausewitz describes as the "fog and friction" of war. The old framework of war does capture that fog and friction are obstacles that affect the conduct of war. However, it incorrectly advises the commander to remain responsive to these obstacles. Conversely, the new framework highlights a more proactive approach to fog and friction. As described in

---

[4] Robert Coram. *Boyd: The Fighter Pilot Who Changed the Art of War*, (Boston: Little, Brown, 2002), 328.

Chapter 3, a commander needs to utilize agility to orient and re-orient to the dynamic strategic environment more quickly, which ultimately leads to tighter OODA loops. The objective is to reinforce the magnification of an adversary' uncertainty and reactive state, then penetrate the weakest section of their moral-mental-physical being to disorient their mental images, disrupt their operations, and overload their system.

The inclusion of the proposed revised framework of war in the capstone joint doctrine guidance document would provide a rubric of warfare, guiding the revision of current joint and service doctrine to address the impacts of the cyber military revolution more adequately. There is solid historical precedent for the incorporation of Colonel John Boyd's OODA loop in Joint Publication 1 to guide strategy, doctrine, and operations at the highest levels of warfare.

Boyd and his theories were integral to the development of the United States Army's AirLand Battle doctrine designed to provide the North Atlantic Treaty Organization (NATO) a means to defeat a numerically superior Warsaw Pact force. Dick Cheney, while Secretary of Defense, sought Boyd's advice and directed his recommendations for applying concepts from the philosophy of war into the development of the overall strategy for the Desert Storm air and ground campaigns.[5] Following the attacks of September 11, 2001, Secretary of State Collin Powell invoked Boyd's theory when he said the United States' response would come over multiple fronts with the intent of getting inside the adversaries' decision cycle.[6]

---

[5] Frans Osinga, *Science, Strategy and War: The Strategic Theory of John Boyd.* (Amsterdam: Eburon Academic Publishers, 2005), 5.
[6] Robert Coram. *Boyd: The Fighter Pilot Who Changed the Art of War,* (Boston: Little, Brown, 2002), 446-447.

Dick Cheney, as Vice President of the United States, provided the best advocacy for the wider adoption of Boyd's OODA loop as a framework of war to confront the today's dynamic and complex strategic environment and the multiple future facets of warfare possible:

> We could use him [Boyd] again now. I wish he was around now. I'd love to turn him loose on our current defense establishment and see what he would come up with. We are still oriented towards the past. We need to think about the next one hundred years rather the last one hundred years.[7]

As this thesis illustrates, we can still "turn Boyd loose" to produce a significant impact on the complex challenges presented by constantly evolving capabilities in the age of cyber warfare. In a April 3, 2012, White Paper on Mission Command, General Dempsey, the Chairman of the Joint Chiefs of Staff, recently reinforced the need to incorporate more of Boyd's concepts into our decision making processes. General Dempsey's paper highlights that today's incredibly dynamic strategic environment will only get more complex as we attempt to anticipate and prepare for the challenges the Joint Force 2020 will face. Commanders will need a process that fosters rapid understanding of the problem and provides quick orientation to define the necessary operational design for achieving the desired end-state:

> Mental agility and superior speed in competitive cycles of decision-making are therefore attributes desired in the commanders of each echelon of the Joint Force 2020. Air Force officer and military strategist John Boyd famously captured the idea that decision-making occurs in recurring cycles of observe-orient-decide-act-the "OODA loop." The key to victory in Colonel Boyd's thinking was the ability to create situations wherein one can make appropriate decisions more quickly than one's opponent.

---

[7]Ibid., 447.

The practice of mission command in the Joint Force 2020 is in this spirit.[8]

Boyd's OODA loop provides the necessary underpinning for both the Joint Force 2020 and a new/revised strategic doctrine. It also closes the conceptual gap in the current framework that operations in the cyber domain have introduced. Most importantly, this revised framework of war also provides the necessary foundation to guide the employment of the United States' strategic capabilities in both the physical and virtual domains.

---

[8] U.S. Joint Chiefs of Staff. *Mission Command White Paper*. (Washington DC: Joint Chiefs of Staff, April 3, 2012), 4.

BIBLIOGRAPHY

Books:

Alexander, Bevin. *Sun Tzu at Gettysburg: Ancient Military Wisdom in the Modern World*. New York: W.W. Norton & Co, 2011.

Andress, Jason, Steve Winterfeld, and Russ Rogers. *Cyber Warfare: Techniques, Tactics and Tools for Security Practitioners*. Amsterdam: Syngress/Elsevier, 2011.

Birla, Madan. *FedEx Delivers: How the World's Leading Shipping Company Keeps Innovating and Outperforming the Competition*. Hoboken, N.J.: John Wiley & Sons, 2005.

Bacevich, A.J., *The Pentomic ERA: The US Army Between Korea and Vietnam*, Washington DC, NDU Press, 1986.

Brenner, Joel. *America the Vulnerable: Inside the New Threat Matrix of Digital Espionage, Crime, and Warfare*. New York: Penguin Press, 2011.

Buckingham, Marcus, and Curt Coffman. *First, Break All the Rules: What the World's Greatest Managers Do Differently*. New York, NY.: Simon & Schuster, 1999.

Carr, Jeffrey, and Lewis Shepherd. *Inside Cyber Warfare*. Sebastopol, Calif: O'Reilly Media, Inc, 2010.

Christensen, Clayton M. *The Innovator's Dilemma: The Revolutionary Book That Will Change the Way You Do Business*. New York: HarperCollins, 2003.

Clarke, Richard A., and Robert K. Knake. *Cyber War: The Next Threat to National Security and What to Do About It*. New York: Ecco, 2010.

Clausewitz, Carl von, Michael Howard, and Peter Paret. *On war*. Princeton, N.J.: Princeton University Press, 1976.

Coram, Robert. *Boyd: The Fighter Pilot Who Changed the Art of War*. Boston: Little, Brown, 2002.

Dunnigan, James F. *The Next War Zone: Confronting the Global Threat of Cyberterrorism*. New York: Citadel Press, 2002.

Dyer, Jeff, Hal B. Gregersen, and Clayton M. Christensen. *The Innovator's DNA: Mastering the Five Skills of Disruptive Innovators*. Boston, Mass: Harvard Business Press, 2011.

Friedman, George. *America's Secret War: Inside the Hidden Worldwide Struggle between America and Its Enemies.* New York: Doubleday, 2004.

Ghonim, Wael. Revolution 2.0: *The Power of the People is Greater than the People in Power: A Memoir.* New York: Houghton Mifflin Harcourt, 2012.

Griffith, Samuel B. *Sun Tzu: The Art of War.* New York: Oxford, 1963.

Hammes, Thomas X. *The Sling and the Stone: On War in the 21st Century.* St. Paul, MN: Zenith Press, 2004.

Hammond, Grant T. *The Mind of War: John Boyd and American Security.* Washington DC: Smithsonian, 2001.

Handel, Michael I. *Masters of War.* London: Routledge, 2005.

Kramer, Franklin D., Stuart H. Starr, and Larry K. Wentz. *Towards a (Preliminary) Theory of Cyberpower.* Ft. Belvoir: Defense Technical Information Center, 2008.

Knox, MacGregor, and Williamson Murray. *The Dynamics of Military Revolution, 1300-2050.* Cambridge, UK: Cambridge University Press, 2001.

Kramer, Franklin D., Stuart H. Starr, and Larry K. Wentz. *Cyberpower and National Security.* Washington, D C: National Defense University Press, 2009.

Leonhard, Robert R. *The Principles of War for the Information Age.* Novato, CA: Presidio, 1998.

Osinga, Frans. *Science, Strategy and War: The Strategic Theory of John Boyd.* Amsterdam: Eburon Academic Publishers, 2005.

Ranadivé, Vivek, and Kevin Maney. *The Two-Second Advantage: How We Succeed by Anticipating the Future-- Just Enough.* New York: Crown Business, 2011.

Richards, Chester W. *Certain to Win: The Strategy of John Boyd, Applied to Business.* [Philadelphia, Pa.]: Xlibris, 2004.

Rumelt, Richard P. *Good Strategy, Bad Strategy: The Difference and Why It Matters.* New York: Crown Business, 2011.

Smith, Rupert. *The Utility of Force: The Art of War in the Modern World.* New York: Knopf, 2007.

Tarr, David W. *American Strategy in the Nuclear Age.* New York: MacMillian, 1966.

Toffler, Alvin, and Heidi Toffler. *War and Anti-War: Survival at the Dawn of the 21st Century*. Boston: Little, Brown, 1993.

Van Creveld, Martin. *Technology and War – From 2000 BC to Present*. New York: Free Press, 1989.

Van Creveld, Martin. *The Transformation of War*. New York: Free Press, 1991.

JOURNALS:

Alexander, Keith B. "Building a New Command in Cyberspace" Strategic Studies Quarterly (Summer 2011): 3-12.

Kaldor, Mary. "Inconclusive Wars: Is Clausewitz Still Relevant in these Global Times?" Global Policy Volume 1, Issue 3 (October 2010): 271-281.

Meilinger, Phillip S. "Clausewitz's bad advice," Air Forces Journal (August 2008)

Sheldon, John B. "Deciphering Cyberpower," Strategic Studies Quarterly (Summer 2011): 95-112.

Schuurman, Bart, "Clausewitz and the "New Wars" Scholars," Parameters (Spring 2010): 89-100.

DISSERTATIONS:

Greenwald, Bryon. "Understanding Change: An Intellectual and Practical Study of Military Innovation-U.S. Army Antiaircraft Artillery and the Battle for Legitimacy, 1917-45" PhD diss Ohio State University 2004.

JOINT PUBLICATIONS:

U.S. Joint Chiefs of Staff. *Doctrine for the Armed Forces of the United States*. Joint Publication 1. Washington DC: Joint Chiefs of Staff, 02 May 2007 Incorporating Change 20 March 2009.

U.S. Joint Chiefs of Staff. *Doctrine for Joint Operations*. Joint Publication 3-0. Washington DC: Joint Chiefs of Staff, August 11, 2011.

U.S. Joint Chiefs of Staff. *Mission Command White Paper*. Washington DC, 2012

U.S. Department of Defense. *Strategy for Operating in Cyberspace*. Washington, DC: Department of Defense, 2011.

U.S. Department of Defense. *Sustaining U.S. Global Leadership: Priorities for 21st Century Defense*. Washington, DC, 2012.

.

U.S. President. *Cyberspace Policy Review: Assuring a Trusted and Resilient Information and Communications Infrastructure* Washington, DC: Executive Branch, 2009.

WEBSITES:

Aviation Week. "Israeli used Electronic Attack in Air Strike against Syrian Mystery Target." Aviation Week. http://www.aviationweek.com/aw/generic/story_generic.jsp?channel=awst&id=news/aw100807p2.xml (accessed December 2, 2011).

Barrett, Devlin, "U.S. Outgunned in Hacker War," WSJ.com, http://online.wsj.com/article/SB100014240527023041771045773077733261800 32.html?mod=WSJ_hp_MIDDLENexttoWhatsNewsSecond, (accessed March 28, 2012).

Bassford, Christopher. "Teaching the Clausewitzian Trinity,"Clausewitz.com, http://www.clausewitz.com/readings/Bassford/Trinity/TrinityTeachingNote.htm (accessed February 13, 2012).

Beyerchen, Alan D. "Clausewitz, Nonlinearity, and the Importance of Imagery," Clausewitz.com, http://www.clausewitz.com/readings/Beyerchen/BeyerschenNonlinearity2.pdf, (accessed February 10, 2012).

Boyd, John. "Patterns of Conflict," DNI.net, http://www.dnipogo.org/boyd/patterns_ppt.pdf (accessed February 21, 2012).

Clayton, Mark. "Stuxnet: Ahmadinejad admits cyberweapon hit Iran nuclear program," Christian Science Monitor, http://www.csmonitor.com/USA/2010/1130/Stuxnet-Ahmadinejad-admits-cyberweapon-hit-Iran-nuclear-program, (accessed 29 January 2012).

CWZ, "FBI expert calls for cyber warfare," CWZ.com, http://www.cyberwarzone.com/cyberwarfare/fbi-expert-calls-cyber-warfare?utm_source=twitterfeed&utm_medium=twitter, (accessed March 5, 2012).

Dambrot ,Stuart Mason. "The future cometh: Science, technology and humanity at Singularity Summit 2011 (Part I)," PHYSORG.com, http://www.physorg.com/news/2011-12-future-cometh-science-technology-humanity.html (accessed February 3, 2012).

Fulghum, David A. "Why Syria's Air Defense Systems Failed to Detect Israelis." Aviation Week, http://www.aviationweek.com/aw/blogs/defense/index.jsp?plckController=Blog&plckBlogPage=BlogViewPost&newspaperUserId=27ec4a53-dcc8-42d0-bd3a-01329aef79a7&plckPostId=Blog%3a27ec4a53-dcc8-42d0-bd3a-01329aef79a7Post%3a2710d024-5eda-416c-b117-ae6d649146cd&plckScript=blogScript&plckElementId=blogDest (accessed December 2, 2011).

Follath, Erich and Holger Stark, "The Story of Operation Orchard," Spiegel, http://www.spiegel.de/international/world/0,1518,658663,00.html (accessed December 2, 2011).

Global Security, "Operation Cast Lead," Global Security.org, http://www.globalsecurity.org/military/world/war/operation-cast-lead.htm (accessed November 29, 2011).

Ghannam, Jeff. "Social Media in the Arab World: Leading up to the Uprisings of 2011," Center for International Media Assistance, http://cima.ned.org/sites/default/files/CIMA-Arab_Social_Media-Report%20-%2010-25-11.pdf (accessed January 17, 2012).

Geers, Kenneth. "Sun Tzu and Cyber War," Cooperative Cyber Defence Centre of Excellence, http://www.ccdcoe.org/articles/2011/Geers_SunTzuandCyberWar.pdf, (Accessed February 16, 2012).

Katz, Yaakov. "Stuxnet virus set back Iran's nuclear program by 2 years," Jerusalem ost, http://www.jpost.com/IranianThreat/News/Article.aspx?id=199475 (accessed January 29, 2012).

Keck, Zachary. "Panetta: Cyber attack could paralyze our country," Examiner.com, http://www.examiner.com/foreign-policy-in-washington-dc/panetta-cyber-attack-could-paralyze-our-country (accessed January 7, 2012).

King, James. "OODA Loops for fighter pilots, business analysts and testers." Kingsinsight.com, http://kingsinsight.com/2012/02/27/ooda-loops-for-fighter-pilots-business-analysts-and-testers/, (accessed February 27, 2012).

Knowledge@Wharton, "In the Middle East, Cyberattacks are Flavored with Political Rhetoric," Knowledge@Wharton, http://knowledge.wharton.upeen.edu/arabic/article.cfm?articleid=2774 (accessed January 23, 2012).

Kurzweil, Ray. "The Law of Accelerating Returns," Kurzweil Accelerating Intelligence, http://www.kurzweilai.net/the-law-of-accelerating-returns (accessed February 3, 2012).

Lennon, Mike. "Threat from Cyber Attack Nearing Statistical Certainty," Security Week.com, http://www.securityweek.com/threat-cyber-attacks-nearing-statistical-certainty, (Accessed February 16, 2012).

McConnell, Mike. "Mike McConnell on how to win the cyber war we're losing," Washington Post. http://www.washingtonpost.com/wp-dyn/content/article/2010/02/25/AR2010022502493.html (accessed January 7, 2012).

Nayab, N. "Exploring the OODA Loop with Examples," Bright Hub, http://www.brighthub.com/office/project-management/articles/105998.aspx, (accessed February 24, 2012).

Schectman, Gregory M. "Manipulating the OODA Loop: The Overlooked Role of Information Resource Management in Information Warfare," Maxwell AFB, http://www.au.af.mil/au/awc/awcgate/afit/schec_gm.pdf (accessed February 26, 2012).

TDAXP, Ph.D, "Variations of the OODA Loops 2, The Naive Boydian Loop," TDAXP.com, http://www.tdaxp.com/archive/2006/05/31 (accessed February 21, 2012).

Tarantola, Andrew, "Iran Denies It's Shutting Down the Internet in August, Merely Building a New One Next March," Gizmodo.com, http://gizmodo.com/5900876/iran-denies-its-shutting-down-the-Internet-in-august-merely-building-a-new-one-next-march, (accessed April 14, 2012).

The Next Web, "Middle East, Part of the Next Web Family," The Next Web, http://thenextweb.com/me/2012/01/18/everything-you-need-to-know-about-the-ongoing-israeli-saudi-hacker-struggle/ (accessed January 23, 2012).

VITA

Mark L. Williamson
Lieutenant Colonel
U.S. Air Force

Lt Col Mark Williamson is a 1992 graduate of the U.S. Air Force Academy and received a Bachelor of Science degree in Political Science. His assignments include positions as RC-135 and RQ-4 Instructor and Evaluator pilot and Squadron Commander. He has served on the Headquarters Air Force staff in the A-2 Directorate. He has also served as a deployed Squadron Commander and Deputy Operations Group commander for Operations IRAQI and ENDURING FREEDOM. His most recent assignment was Commander of the 1st Reconnaissance Squadron at Beale AFB, CA.

He is a Distinguished Graduate of the KC-135 Formal Training Unit and Squadron Officers School at Maxwell AFB, AL. He is currently attending the Joint Advanced Warfighting School at the Joint Forces Staff College at Norfolk NAS, VA.